BUSINESS & MANAGEMENT

Revision Workbook

Paul Hoang

First published in 2009 by IBID Press, Victoria.

36 Quail Crescent

Melton 3337

Victoria, Australia

National Library of Australia Cataloguing-in-Publication data:

> Hoang, P.
> 1. Business & Management.
> 2. International Baccalaureate. Series Title: International Baccalaureate in Detail.
> ISBN-13: 978-1-876659-93-6
> ISBN-10: 1-876659-93-9
> First impression 2009.

All possible endeavours have been made by the publishers to ensure that the contents of this resource are correct and appropriate. However, the publishers accept no responsibility for any errors made by the author. The contents and materials are solely the responsibility of the author.

IBID Press would like to sincerely thank the International Baccalaureate Organization for permission to reproduce its intellectual property.

This material has been developed independently by the publisher and the content is in no way connected with nor endorsed by the International Baccalaureate Organization.

Cover design by Adcore.

Printed by Trojan Press Pty. Ltd.

Contents

Contents

Contents

Message from the author

Dear students (and teachers),

I hope that you find this *Business & Management Revision Workbook* to be of value in preparing you for reviewing your learning of Business & Management.

There are several ways that you can use the Revision Workbook:

- To review the units that you have studied with your teachers in class
- As end of topic tests – set by your teachers or as part of your self assessment – during the two-year course
- As a revision tool prior to the final examinations.

The solutions to the questions are included in the enclosed CD-ROM to aid your revision and learning. However, *please* be disciplined and refrain from seeking the answers before you have attempted the questions (making mistakes is an essential part of the learning process!). Most, if not all, of the answers should come from your reading of the textbook *Business & Management*, also published by IBID Press.

Finally, please allow me the opportunity to wish you the best for your forthcoming examinations.

Paul Hoang

paulhoang88@hotmail.com

* * * * * * * *

Dedicated to the students of Sha Tin College, Hong Kong

* * * * * * * *

BUSINESS ORGANIZATION AND ENVIRONMENT

UNIT 1

Unit 1.1   Nature of Business Activity

Task 1: Complete the missing words

A .... is an organization that uses inputs, known as factors of ...., to produce goods and services. .... are physical products, such as pens, televisions and clothing. .... are intangible products such as education, health care and foreign holidays. .... is the process of using factor inputs (also known as the .... of ....) to generate the .... of either a good or service. These are then purchased by .... (people or businesses that buy the product) and then used by the .... (the end user, be it a business or a person).

Task 2: Vocabulary quiz

a   Identify the correct stage of production from the clues below.

Stage of Production	Description
	Transformation of primary resources into manufactured goods for sale
	Extraction of natural resources such as farming and mining
	Provision of services such as distribution and after-sales care

b   Find the correct factor of production from the given definitions.

Factor of Production	Definition
	An individual who has the skills and ability to take risks in organizing the other three factors of production to generate output in a profitable way
	All natural resources that are used in the production process, e.g. wood, water, physical land and minerals
	Non-natural or manufactured resources used to further the production process, e.g. money, buildings, machinery, tools and vehicles
	Physical human effort and psychological intellect used in the production process

c   Identify the correct functional department in each case below.

Functional Department	Functional Roles
	Prepares accounts such as profit and loss accounts and balance sheets and manages the money of the business
	Manufactures goods in order to meet quality standards, targets and deadlines
	Conducts research to meet the needs of customers and arranges promotional activities to sell the firm's products
	Handles recruitment, training and the general welfare of the workforce

Task 3: Explain …

a   Three advantages of specialization

_____

_____

_____

b   Two disadvantages of specialization

_____

_____

c   Three qualities of successful entrepreneurs

_____

_____

_____

Task 4: Multiple choice

1   The resources used in the production process are collectively known as
   A Human capital resources
   B Raw materials
   C Working capital
   D Factors of production

2   Specialization does *not* benefit from
   A Monotony of doing same job
   B Productivity from specialization
   C Products that are mass produced
   D Increased competitiveness

3   The difference between the cost of the inputs in the production process and the price of the final output is known as
   A Income
   B Revenue
   C Added value
   D Profit

4   Which of the following is *not* an example of primary production?
   A Agriculture
   B Fishing
   C Mining
   D Coaching

5   Which occupation does *not* exist in the tertiary sector?
   A Estate agent
   B Secretary
   C Machinist
   D Librarian

6   The primary sector is the part of the economy that consists of

   A   Agriculture, fishing and extractive industries

   B   Little, if any, government control

   C   Businesses that have been recently set up

   D   Organizations that lack finance

7   The secondary sector

   A   Forms the largest employment sector in most developed countries

   B   Provides both goods and services

   C   Consists of businesses involved in the manufacturing of goods

   D   Is labour intensive

8   Production is

   A   The process of making goods and services from the available factors inputs

   B   The manufacturing of goods in the secondary industry

   C   Any output other than services

   D   The second stage of the output process

9   The advantages of specialization include all those listed except

   A   A greater amount of output

   B   Development of expertise and skills

   C   Wider choice of options for customers

   D   Increase in overall efficiency of production

10   Which of the following businesses would *not* be described as operating in the tertiary sector?

   A   Pest control

   B   Restaurant

   C   Private security

   D   Textiles

11   The process of increasing the value of a resource in the production process is known as

   A   Adding value

   B   Chain of production

   C   Production function

   D   Value chain analysis

12   Computers are an example of which type of factor input?

   A   Labour

   B   Land

   C   Capital

   D   Machinery

13   Which of the following is the least specialized?

   A   Lawyer of criminal law

   B   Taxi driver

   C   Primary school teacher

   D   Professional basketball player

14 Public utilities, such as water and gas supply, are usually considered as being in the tertiary sector because they

    A Are owned by the government

    B Provide services to the general public

    C Are involved with turning resources into a useable product

    D Are not extracted or manufactured

15 The term 'product' refers to

    A Services only

    B Goods only

    C Both goods and services

    D The physical attributes of a good

16 The ………….. sector of the economy is owned by individuals and companies, usually in pursuit of making profit. The ………….. sector is controlled by the government that aims primarily to provide a service by acting in the public's best interest.

    A Private, Public

    B Public Private

    C Primary, Tertiary

    D Tertiary, Primary

17 Which of the following would *not* be regarded as part of the tertiary sector?

    A Leisure and tourism

    B Insurance

    C Education and training

    D Engineering

18 The division of labour is most extensively observed in which of the following case?

    A Original oil paintings

    B Made-to-measure suits

    C Lecturing at University

    D Hairdressing

19 As factors of production, which of the following is *not* classed as land?

    A Fish

    B Paper

    C Water

    D Crude oil

20 An entrepreneur is someone who:

    A Owns a business as a sole trader or as the primary shareholder

    B Organizes factor inputs and takes the risks in business decisions

    C Is an industrialist who manages production and output

    D Has a managerial or supervisory role within an organization

Unit 1.2   Types of Organization

Task 1: Complete the missing words

A ………… ……….… is a business owned and run by a single person. Such firms are very common partly because there are few legal procedures involved in setting up the business. The owner bears all the risks of running the business but has full ………..… and gets to reap all ………..… that the business makes. However, the owner also has……………...… ………..…, meaning that s/he may need to sell personal possessions in order to meet any debts that the business may encounter.

An ordinary ……………...… is an alliance of between 2 and 20 individual owners who are jointly responsible for the affairs of the business. The joint owners will usually sign a mutually agreed contract known as the …………..… …. …………..…….. Most, if not all, of the partners in the business face unlimited liability for any debts the business might incur. Partners that simply place their money into the business as an investment but without any direct involvement in the business are known as …………..… …………..… These partners enjoy limited liability.

Limited companies are owned by ……………...… who have limited liability. This is because all limited companies are ……………..… businesses, i.e. the organizations are treated as a separate legal identity from their owners. Shareholders get one ……….. for each share that they hold in the company. …………..… limited companies tend to be relatively small companies that are owned by family members. In order to become a …………..… limited company, the firm has to sell shares to the public for the first time, known as an …………..… …………..… …………..… (IPO). In return for their investment, shareholders are given a proportion of the company's profits (if any) in the form of …………..… payments, which are usually paid …………..… a year. The declared payment is paid on each share that a shareholder owns, so the more shares held the higher the total payout will be. Shareholders also buy shares in the hope that there is a …………..… …………..…, i.e. the share price rises.

Task 2: Vocabulary quiz

Identify the key terms from the clues given. *Hint*: the answers are in alphabetical order.

Key Term	Definition
	Altruistic businesses that operate predominantly in the private sector with the objectives of a promoting a worthwhile cause
	Term used to describe a private limited company offering its shares on the stock exchange, thereby changing its legal status to a public limited company
	Private sector businesses that do not primarily aim to make a profit for its owners
	The sale of public sector organizations or assets to private individuals and companies, thereby transferring these to private sector ownership
	Sector in which businesses are run and owned by the government in order to provide communal services for society, e.g. state education and health care
	An investor in a partnership that does not get involved in the day to day management of the business
	The marketplace for buying and selling second-hand company stocks and shares
	The limitless amount of debt that the owner(s) of a business can incur if things do not go well

Task 3: True or false?

		True / False
a	A public limited company can advertise its shares and have them quoted on a stock exchange.	
b	The liability of shareholders is limited to the amount of their investment.	
c	All businesses have an aim to make profit for their owners.	
d	Survival is the main aim of businesses in the long term.	
e	A Stock Exchange represents the market where second-hand shares can be bought and sold.	
f	Public corporations are also known as public companies.	
g	A not-for-profit organization is any organization that does not primarily aim to make a profit.	
h	Public companies are examples of private sector businesses.	
i	All non-governmental organizations (NGOs) operate in the private sector.	
j	'Limited liability' means that if a firm is unable to pay back its debts, the owners of the business can lose everything, including their personal possessions.	
k	Pressure groups can constrain as well as foster business activity.	

Task 4: Explain one ...

a   Benefit of staying small as a business

b   Purpose of companies holding an Annual General Meeting (AGM)

c   Feature of the private sector

d   Difference between a Public Corporation and a Public Company

e   Advantage of being a private limited company

Task 5: Multiple choice

1   A sole trader is a person who

    A Sets up the safest form of business organization

    B Has exclusive responsibility for the running of the business

    C Is not legally liable for any debts of the business

    D Forms a business with another single person

2   In comparison to other forms of business, sole proprietors face the problem of

    A Specialization

    B Continuity

    C Administration and set up procedures

    D Privacy of account

3   Advantages of sole traders do *not* include

    A Flexibility and freedom in decision making

    B Profits not having to be shared with others

    C A high degree of confidentiality in administration and financial reporting

    D The various sources of finance available

4   Disadvantages of sole traders exclude

    A The demands of having to be multi-skilled

    B A reliance on the efforts and liability of just one person

    C Constraint of lack of time and specialization

    D Autonomy in decision making

5   Which of the following is *not* a necessary condition for an ordinary partnership?

    A Signing the contents of a partnership deed

    B Having between 2–20 partners

    C Having at least one partner with unlimited liability

    D Shares cannot be issued by the business

6   The legal document that sets out the constitution of a limited company is known as the

    A Memorandum of Association

    B Articles of Association

    C Deed of Incorporation

    D Certificate of Incorporation

7   The document that outlines the purpose of a new business and its plans for business success is known as the

    A Business plan

    B Memorandum of Association

    C Articles of Association

    D Annual Report

8   Which statement does *not* apply to charities?

    A They are not-for-profit organizations

    B They promote and raise money for good causes

    C They are private sector businesses

    D They are registered as having limited liability

9 Which of the statements is false?

  A A private limited company cannot sell its shares on a stock exchange

  B Second-hand shares of public companies can be traded on a stock exchange

  C Public limited companies operate in the private sector

  D The Board of Directors of a private limited company own the business

10 Which of the statements about shareholders is correct?

  A As co-owners of a corporation, they have equal voting rights

  B An advantage for shareholders is having limited liability

  C They own and control private and public limited companies

  D They are always given dividends twice a year as their return for investing in a company

11 The Memorandum of Association

  A States the main purpose of a company

  B Stipulates the internal functions and rules of an organization

  C Shows how profits will be distributed to its owners

  D Sets out rules for the appointment and remuneration of directors

12 Identify the incorrect statement below.

  A Public companies operate in the public sector

  B Silent Partner is another name for sleeping partner

  C A Deed of Partnership is advised as it helps to resolve disagreements

  D Shareholders are not personally liable for the debts of their business

13 The shareholders of a company

  A Are wealthier than sole traders or partners

  B All have voting rights

  C Are legally entitled to a share of company profits

  D Control the running of the business

14 Which of the following is least likely to be a non-profit organization?

  A Museums

  B Performing arts groups

  C Police force

  D Public transport firms

15 Which of the following is *not* a pressure group?

  A World Wildlife Fund

  B Oxfam International

  C National Union of Teachers

  D Non-executive directors of a company

16 Unincorporated means that a business

  A Has shareholders

  B Has unlimited liability for its debts

  C Is a separate legal entity from its owners

  D Is owned by one person

17 Which of the following is *not* a reason why people may choose to set up their own business?

   A There are higher risks than working for someone else

   B To enjoy autonomy in decision making

   C To extend personal interests and hobbies

   D A lack of employment opportunities

18 The Memorandum of Association states

   A The liability of a business and the amount of capital invested

   B The registered address of the business and names of all directors and shareholders

   C That an incorporated business is able to start trading as a limited company

   D That liability of shareholders is limited to the amount of capital invested in the company

19 Which statement does *not* apply to sole traders?

   A The business is owned by one person

   B There may be more than one employee

   C There can be more than one employer

   D It is the most common form of ownership

20 Which of the following is least likely to be classed as a non-profit organization?

   A Private fee paying schools or colleges

   B Charities

   C Pressure groups

   D Consultancy services

21 Which of the following is least likely to be a disadvantage of a partnership?

   A Having to share profits

   B Dealing with different sources of finance

   C Less control of business activities

   D Managing conflict and disagreements

22 A public sector enterprise is

   A An organization owned by the state or government

   B An organization owned by shareholders who can trade their shares on a stock exchange

   C An organization owned by private shareholders only

   D Any business that carries 'Ltd' or 'Plc' after its name

23 Which document is issued to a limited company before it can start trading?

   A Memorandum of Association

   B Deed of Partnership

   C Certificate of Incorporation

   D Articles of Association

24 A non-profit organization that operates in the private sector and runs for the benefit of others in society is known as a

   A Charity

   B Non-governmental organization

   C Non-profit organization

   D Not-for-profit organization

25 The process of selling or transferring state-owned organizations to the private sector is known as
   A Liquidation
   B Privatization
   C Transference
   D Sale and transfer

26 What is the other name for a public limited company?
   A Joint stock company
   B Private sector company
   C Private limited company
   D Public corporation

27 A public sector corporation is an organization that
   A Is owned by the government
   B Issues shares to the general public on the stock exchange
   C Seeks to make profit as its main objective
   D Has limited liability

28 A drawback of public limited companies is that they
   A Have limited liability
   B Have to publish certain financial information to all stakeholders
   C Rely on government funding
   D Represent high risks to investors

29 Which of the following is an example of public (sector) expenditure?
   A Investment by public limited companies
   B Donations made to charities and non-profit organizations
   C Spending on state education and health care
   D Spending by the general public on company stocks and shares

30 Charities get their finance from different sources. Which one is the exception?
   A Donations
   B Running fund-raising events
   C Selling products
   D Corporation tax refunds

Unit 1.3 Organizational Objectives

Task 1: Complete the missing words

The .... of a business are concerned with its long-term goals and stem from an organization's .... statement. Hence, aims are a general statement of a firm's intentions, e.g. to expand into overseas markets. Aims tend to be .... rather than quantitative in nature.

A business will tend to find it difficult to satisfy all its stakeholders simultaneously due to their own c.................... objectives. For example, shareholders are likely to demand that the business aims for .... maximization whilst employees will strive to maximize their own .... and benefits (thereby potentially reducing the profits of the business).

Organizations are increasingly concerned with the possible impact of their actions on the environment and society. This is largely because of the increased public awareness and concern for the planet's natural environment. Adverse business activity could lead to unwanted publicity from pressure groups. Such negative exposure can destroy customer .... and the .... of the business. Unethical business practices might also adversely affect the firm's suppliers, employees, creditors and investors. Ultimately, ignoring ethics and social .... can seriously harm a firm's profitability. Hence, there are ever more driving forces pushing businesses to behave in a socially responsible way.

Task 2: Match the terms

Read the definitions and match them with the correct business terms from the list below.

	Term		Definition
a	Strategy	i	The long-term goals of a business that provide direction for setting its objectives and targets
b	Aims	ii	This declaration sets out the vision of an organization to provide a shared purpose and direction for all those involved in the firm
c	Mission statement	iii	Refers to the obligations that a business has towards its stakeholders and society as a whole
d	Objectives	iv	The medium-term to long-term actions of a business (what needs to be done, the resources needed to do it and the time frame in which to accomplish it) in order to achieve its aims and objectives
e	Social responsibility	v	The (very) long-term desire or aspiration of an organization
f	Vision	vi	The medium-term to long-term goals and targets of an organization, e.g. survival, diversification and growth

Task 3: Odd one out

Select the odd one out from each of the options below.

a	Tactical objectives	Operational objectives	Strategic objectives	Secondary objectives
b	Growth	Sales maximization	Survival	Acquisition
c	To control	To select	To direct	To motivate
d	To improve quality of customer service	To become the world's market leader	To reduce absenteeism and labour turnover	To improve productive efficiency

Task 4: True or false?

		True / False
a	If a business behaves ethically, its profits will fall in the short run.	
b	A business that adopts an ethical approach will tend to improve its profits in the long run.	
c	Strategic objectives refer to the general organizational objectives of a business that encompass its long-term goals.	
d	A business that has an ethical policy in the workplace is said to have an ethical stance.	
e	The amount of recycling that a firm undertakes is likely to be reported in the firm's social audit.	
f	All businesses in the private sector aim to make profit whereas those operating in the public sector aim primarily to provide a service to the general public.	
g	For most businesses, the objectives of shareholders are more important than those of other stakeholders.	
h	Being socially responsible is the same as being environmentally responsible.	
i	Ethical corporate responsibility considers the welfare of the workforce.	
j	The overall purpose of an organization can often be seen from its mission statement.	

Task 5: Explain …

a   Why a business might choose to act unethically

_____

_____

b   The purpose of producing an ethical code of practice in the workplace

_____

_____

c   Why a business might choose to donate money to charitable organizations

_____

_____

d   Whether polluting the environment is legal, illegal or unethical in your country

_____

_____

e   Why organizational objectives should be agreed through a process of consultation with employees rather than simply being set by senior management

_____

_____

Task 6: Multiple choice

1   The declaration of the future identity of a business is known as its

    A   Business objectives

    B   Corporate identity

    C   Mission statement

    D   Vision statement

2   What is the concept used to describe what an organization is in business for and what it intends to achieve?

    A   Business plan

    B   Business objectives

    C   Mission statement

    D   Vision statement

3   Objectives are

    A   What a business wants to achieve

    B   The purpose for a firm's existence

    C   Qualitative statements of a firm's direction

    D   The major goals of an organization

4   Possible objectives of public sector organizations are least likely to include:

    A   To provide a service to the community

    B   To survive

    C   To break-even as soon as possible

    D   To maximize levels of profit

5   Advantages of setting ethical objectives do *not* include

    A   Avoiding bad publicity

    B   An obligation to provide shareholder dividends

    C   A possible unique selling point of the firm

    D   Impact on staff morale

6   Businesses do not always consider acting in an ethical way. Which of the following does *not* explain why this might be the case?

    A   Ethical objectives often conflict with profit objectives

    B   There might not be any government constraints

    C   Compliance costs are low

    D   Ethics might not be important to the firm

7   A social audit does not include a firm's

    A   Financial performance

    B   Use of recycled materials

    C   Treatment of the workforce

    D   Waste disposal processes

8 Which of the following is *not* an example of ethical policies adopted by a business?

  A Fringe benefits offered to all members of staff

  B Sponsoring charity events in the local community

  C Fair trading terms with businesses in less economically developed countries

  D The safe disposal of waste materials

9 Many businesses strive to be the market leader. Which of the following methods is least likely to achieve this objective?

  A Maintain customer satisfaction

  B Competitive prices

  C Maintain product quality

  D Have high labour turnover

10 A code of practice is *not* likely to include details concerning

  A Social responsibilities

  B Expectations of employees in the workplace

  C Ethical marketing

  D Statutory employment rights

11 Objectives do *not*

  A Provide a focus for the workforce

  B Help to assess the performance of a business

  C Suggest how goals should be achieved

  D Inform strategic planning

12 What details might *not* be included in a social audit?

  A Ethical marketing practices

  B Treatment of employees

  C Defect rates

  D Accident rates

13 The process by which a business reviews and evaluates the effect of its activities on all of its stakeholders is known as

  A An ethical code of practice

  B Social corporate responsibility

  C Social auditing

  D Environmental auditing

14 Unethical business practices do *not* include

  A Setting higher prices to raise profit margins

  B The production of demerit goods such as alcohol and tobacco

  C Lending money to companies that make war weapons

  D Deliberately using offensive tactics to marketing a firm's products

15 What does the 'R' in SMART objectives stand for?

  A Realistic

  B Rational

  C Reasonable

  D Righteous

Unit 1.4 Stakeholders

Task 1: Complete the missing words

Stakeholders are ……………….., groups or organizations that have a direct interest in the performance of a ……………….. or are directly affected by the operations of the business. Examples include: ……………….., directors, employees, competitors, customers and suppliers.

External stakeholders are those that are not directly involved in a business, but have an interest in the operation of that business. Examples of external stakeholders include the ……………….., the local community and ……………….. groups.

The local community is an example of a ………….. interest group (SIG). Local residents can bring about problems for a business. For example, firms that may offer job opportunities but pollute the local environment and offer ……….. working conditions are likely to face some hostility.

Task 2: Stakeholder groups

Identify the stakeholder group from the given clues regarding that group's main interests. *Hint*: answers appear in *reverse* alphabetical order.

Stakeholder Group	Examples of Stakeholder Group's Interest
	Regular orders and ability to meet payment deadlines
	Regular dividends, higher share prices, discounts for patronage
	Employment opportunities, financial support for events (such as sponsorship deals or charitable donations), minimize disruptions to the environment
	Good remuneration package and job security, safe working environment, opportunities for career development
	Competitive prices, safe and good quality products, after-sales care and overall value for money
	Minimal risk and ability to repay the money owed

Task 3: Explain …

a   The difference between shareholders and stakeholders

_____

_____

b   The difference between directors and shareholders

_____

_____

c   What Bill Gates, founder of Microsoft Corporation, meant by "Your most unhappy customers are your greatest sources of learning".

_____

_____

d   The sources of conflict in large organizations such as British Airways or American Airlines

_____

_____

e   The difference between internal and external stakeholders

_____

_____

Task 4: Multiple choice

1   Stakeholders are

   A People who can influence the behaviour of businesses

   B Individuals, groups or organizations that are affected by the behaviour of businesses

   C All those parties directly working for an organization and are affected by its actions

   D The people or organizations that own shares in the business

2   Which of the following stakeholder groups is classified as an external stakeholder?

   A Owners or shareholders

   B Employees

   C Executive directors

   D Creditors

3   Which of the following stakeholders is least likely to be an external stakeholder?

   A General public

   B Government

   C Trade unions

   D Competitors

4   A business might want to become involved in community projects even though there are not necessarily any direct financial gains from doing so. Which option below does _not_ provide a reason for doing so?

   A The subsequent press coverage that it may attract

   B To enhance the image of the business

   C To boost staff morale and motivation

   D For staff professional development

5   What is the primary role of a trade union?

   A Push for higher wages for staff

   B Represent members in disciplinary and grievance matters

   C Uphold the welfare of members

   D Negotiate contracts with employers for its members

6   An organization of individuals who unite to further their common interest is known as a

   A Labour union

   B Trade organization

   C Pressure group

   D Campaigning group

7 Lobbying groups would *not* typically support

    A The protection of animals

    B Treatment of workers

    C Deforestation

    D Anti-smoking

8 Which of the following is least likely to be an objective of pressure groups?

    A Influence business and consumer behaviour

    B Change government policy

    C Change opinions of the general public

    D Change government macroeconomic objectives

9 Which of the following is a special interest group?

    A Employees

    B Directors

    C Local community

    D Suppliers

10 Internal stakeholders include

    A Stockholders

    B Creditors

    C Debtors

    D Competitors

11 External stakeholders include

    A Customers

    B Shareholders

    C Employees

    D Directors

12 Stakeholders, such as customers and employees, of a socially responsible firm may want the business to donate money to charity. Shareholders of the same firm may not necessarily agree with this since it comes from their potential dividends. This is an example of

    A Compliance costs

    B Shareholder compliance

    C Stakeholder conflict

    D Stakeholder divergence

13 Special interest groups can affect business decision-making in all the following ways except

    A Public protests

    B Lobbying

    C Loitering

    D Direct action

14 How do pressure groups primarily strive to achieve their aims?

    A By raising as much publicity and awareness of their cause as possible

    B By lobbying the government for changes in the law

    C By organizing mass demonstrations to win public support

    D By getting the workforce to take industrial action

15 Which statement below does *not* apply to the shareholders of a business?

    A They are the owners of limited companies

    B They have an interest in the operation and survival of the business

    C They are all internal stakeholders

    D They receive dividends each year based on the number of shares they hold

16 Which of the following is *not* an internal stakeholder of the Industrial and Commercial Bank of China (ICBC)?

    A The management

    B The shareholders

    C The Chinese government

    D The hourly-waged staff at ICBC

17 Stakeholder group X has the following interests: Financial benefits, Job security, Working environment and Continuous professional and development needs. Which stakeholder group is least likely to be X?

    A Managers

    B Directors

    C Employees

    D Entrepreneurs

18 Boycotting is often used by pressure groups to

    A Push governments to introduce legislation desired by the pressure group

    B Create adverse publicity for a business by advocating customers to avoid the business

    C Prevent employees from being able to attend work

    D Taking a business to court for its socially undesirable behaviour

19 What arises because an organization cannot meet the needs of all its stakeholders at the same time?

    A Conflict

    B Miscommunication

    C Mismanagement

    D Lobbying

20 Anti-piracy advertising against the illegal downloading of music and movies would be an example of a campaign promoted by

    A Trade unions

    B Industry trade groups

    C Local communities

    D Pressure groups

Unit 1.5 External Environment

Task 1: Complete the missing words

PEST analysis stands for the ...., ...…............, ..., and ....
factors that affect businesses, all of which are beyond an individual firm's.................. PEST analysis
gives managers an overview of the .... business environment, the factors that might affect
business activity and the issues that should be addressed in any business strategy.

Variations of PEST analysis include: ...., (a more optimistic approach to PEST analysis), STEEPLE
and PESTLE (where the additional letters in PESTLE stand for ...., and ...., and
the additional E is STEEPLE stands for ....).

Task 2: Explain why ...

a The introduction of a national minimum wage may be both a threat and an opportunity for
businesses

_____

_____

b Businesses that do not initiate change are still at risk in the external business environment

_____

_____

c A higher exchange rate can present both opportunities and threats to a domestic business

_____

_____

d Sustainable inflation (which makes prices rise) does not make a person poorer

_____

_____

Task 3: PEST analysis

a The table below shows examples of different external factors that affect businesses. In each case,
identify whether the example is a political (P), economic (E), social (S) or technological (T) factor.
An example has been done for you.

Example	External Factor	Example	External Factor
Ageing population	S	Tariffs and quotas	
Average family size changes		Consumer protection legislation	
Consumer confidence levels		Oil price changes	
E-commerce developments		Scientific development	
Employment legislation		Interest rates changes	
Exchange rate fluctuations		Falling exchange rates	

b   Identify the type of external factors (i.e. the STEEPLE factors) that affect businesses from the clues below.

Type of External Influence	Examples
	Consumers go 'green' and recycle in order to conserve the planet.
	Decision to spend more money on public education and health-care services.
	Increasing number of older and retired people in the country.
	Interest rate hikes dampen purchase of private and commercial property.
	More businesses devote money to developing their e-commerce strategies.
	Smoking bans in restaurants, shopping malls and public parks.

Task 4: True or false?

		True / False
a	Falling rates of inflation will lead to lower prices in the economy.	
b	Inflation will tend to damage a country's international competitiveness.	
c	Deflation is good for the economy as prices are falling, so demand rises.	
d	The Central Bank can boost economic growth by cutting interest rates.	
e	If the exchange rate between pounds sterling and Hong Kong dollars changes from £1 = $15 to £1 = $16, then sterling is said to have strengthened.	
f	France has a maximum working week of 35 hours. This is an example of an economic constraint on businesses.	
g	An appreciation of sterling (£) against the euro (€) will lead to a fall in UK exports to the rest of Europe.	
h	Chinese importers will benefit from bilateral trade if the US dollar appreciates against the Chinese yuan.	
i	A government is likely to raise interest rates during times of inflationary pressure.	
j	If a government attempts to reduce unemployment, then it could consider cutting interest rates.	

Task 5: Vocabulary quiz

All the key terms below refer to external factors that present either threats or opportunities for businesses. Identify the key term from the given definitions. *Hint*: all key terms appear in *reverse* alphabetical order.

Key Term	Definition
	This refers to the series of fluctuations in the GDP of an economy over time. The phases ('recession', 'slump', 'recovery', and 'boom') are dependent on both the level of employment and income and wealth in a country.
	As a form of protectionism, this tax is imposed on imported products. It is levied by a government to reduce the competitiveness of foreign imports.
	This occurs when there has been a decline in the level of economic activity for at least two consecutive quarters (half a year). Features include lower levels of consumption and investment expenditure in the economy.
	This refers to any form of government measure used to defend domestic businesses (and hence jobs) from international competition, e.g. imposing a tariff on foreign imports.
	This is a government macroeconomic policy designed to control the economy by managing the money supply mainly via changes in interest rates and exchange rates.
	This refers to the cost of money to consumers and firms. The higher this is, the lower the amount of borrowing tends to be whilst savings are encouraged. At the same time, firms may delay investment projects due to the higher costs.
	Arguably the most important macroeconomic objective which measures the percentage change in the general price level of a country over the preceding 12 months.
	This is a category of tax that is charged on goods and services, e.g. VAT, GST and excise duties.
	This refers to an increase in the value of a country's total output of goods and services, per time period (usually per year).
	This is a type of tax that is paid directly from the income, wealth or profit of an individual or a business, e.g. income tax and corporation tax respectively.

Task 6: The economic environment

a   Describe how an increase in interest rates should dampen the rate of inflation in the economy.

_____

_____

b   Explain why a higher exchange rate is not necessarily good for the economy.

_____

_____

c   Explain the positive correlation between a change in interest rates and a change in the exchange rate.

_____

_____

d   Outline why inflation might make a country less internationally competitive.

_____

_____

e   Describe how an increase in income tax rates could help to reduce inflationary pressures in a country.

_____

_____

f   Identify the missing labels in the diagram below.

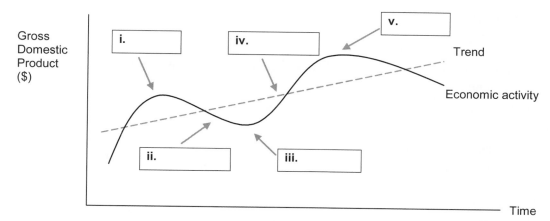

g   Use the data below to calculate the annual rate of inflation. Round your answer to two decimal places and show all your working.

Year	CPI
Year 2	110.0
Year 1	106.5

_____

_____

Task 7: Multiple choice

1   Political factors affecting businesses do *not* directly include

   A   Legislative changes

   B   Import taxes

   C   The government's relationship with other nations

   D   Floating exchange rates

2   Social factors in the external business environment take account of changes in

   A   Exchange rates

   B   Company tax rates

   C   Customs, habits and tastes

   D   Interest rates

3 Economic variables affecting businesses exclude changes in the level of a country's

   A Unemployment

   B Education and training

   C Inflation

   D International trade

4 The study of population structures and population trends and their likely impact on business activity is known as

   A Social-cultural studies

   B Social trends

   C Demography

   D Populace

5 Which of the following strategies could be best used to deal with the problems caused by a short-term recession?

   A Reducing the size of the workforce

   B Moving to cheaper premises

   C Lowering prices to maintain sales

   D Redesign products to cater for income-sensitive customers

6 Deregulation is

   A The removal of controls in a particular industry

   B Imposing regulation to control the activities of businesses

   C Privatizing businesses in the public sector

   D The fall in manufacturing output or employment in the secondary sector

7 'External constraints' include all those listed below except

   A Changes in consumer tastes

   B Social attitudes and cultures

   C External sources of finance

   D Unemployment levels

8 Which of the following is a direct tax?

   A Sales taxes

   B Alcohol, tobacco and petrol taxes

   C Excise duties

   D Taxes on interest and dividends

9 If the exchange rate of the pound sterling (£) changes from £1: $1.60 to £1:$1.80, then the currency is said to have

   A Weakened

   B Strengthened

   C Deflated

   D Floated

10 Which of the following is *not* a valid reason for government intervention in business activity?

    A To encourage competition between firms rather than allowing monopolies to exploit the market

    B To protect consumers through legislation

    C To protect the environment through punishing polluters

    D To supply services such as health care to compete with private sector firms

11 Fiscal policy is about

    A Increasing the level of aggregate demand in an economy

    B Using a Central Bank to alter interest rates

    C Taxation and government spending policy

    D Using exchange rates to affect spending in the economy

12 An ethical business would *not*

    A Pay attention to the natural environment

    B Treat its employees with respect

    C Pay huge bonuses to its board of directors

    D Minimize waste

13 Gross Domestic Product measures

    A The level of real incomes in an economy

    B The amount of production taken place in a country each year

    C The total value of a country's output during a year

    D A change in prices of a representative basket of goods and services

14 The Central Bank of a country has a role in setting the level of

    A Government borrowing

    B Government expenditure

    C Interest rates

    D Taxation

15 Inflation can be caused by

    A A rise in the price of vital imported raw materials

    B An increase in a nation's productivity

    C An increase in a nation's productive capacity

    D A fall in business and consumer confidence levels

16 Which of the following taxes is a direct tax?

    A Goods and Services Tax

    B Corporation Tax

    C Import tariffs

    D Excise Duties

17 Which of the following would *not* be used as a fiscal policy instrument?

    A Reducing income tax rates

    B Reducing interest rates

    C Increasing government spending on schools

    D Reducing the government's budget deficit

18 Which of the following taxes is least likely to directly affect a business in the hotel and catering industry?

    A Corporation tax

    B Excise duties

    C Income tax

    D Local government taxes

19 What is the most likely result of higher interest rates in the economy?

    A An increase in the volume of exports

    B Higher levels of investments

    C Weakened consumer spending

    D More applications for bank loans

20 Study the table below and calculate the amount of direct tax revenue collected by the government:

	$ millions
Corporation tax	52,350
Customs duties	32,550
Excise duties	42,250
Goods and Services Sales tax	63,505
Income tax	245,500

    A $245,500 million

    B $297,850 million

    C $361,355 million

    D $372,650 million

21 If a government wished to stimulate economic growth, which policy would it be most likely to increase?

    A Government spending

    B Income tax

    C Interest rates

    D Exchange rates

22 Which of the following types of unemployment is generally regarded as the least problematic?

    A Cyclical

    B Frictional

    C Regional

    D Structural

23 Which of the following is *not* a stage in the economic trade cycle?

    A Boom

    B Recession

    C Recovery

    D Decline

24 In August 2000, the exchange rate of the British pound to the HK dollar averaged £1 = HK$11.63. By August 2008, it had changed to £1 = HK$14.80. Thus it can be said that during this time the HK dollar had:

    A Not changed in value since the two nations do not use the same currency

    B Appreciated by around 27%

    C Depreciated by around 27%

    D Fallen by around 22%

25 Which of the following is *not* considered to be an external shock?

    A An oil crisis raising the costs of production for most industries

    B The outbreak of war

    C Financial and cash-flow problems harming international expansion plans

    D Higher than expected unemployment causing a fall in domestic sales

26 An increase in the level of unemployment is an example of

    A Demographic change

    B Economic change

    C Social change

    D Political change

27 Employment practices that take a more positive attitude towards women in terms of pay and promotional opportunities is an example of

    A Economic change

    B Demographic change

    C Social change

    D Political change

28 Higher economic growth is most likely to be achieved if there is significantly lower

    A Deflation

    B Inflation

    C Consumption

    D Unemployment

29 Calculate the unemployment rate in a country with a population of 60 million people, of which 30 million are employed and 2 million are unemployed.

    A 3.33%

    B 5.33%

    C 6.25%

    D 6.66%

30 Using the same data for Question 29 above, what is the number of people in the labour force?

    A 28 million

    B 30 million

    C 32 million

    D 60 million

31 A hike in interest rates, all other things remaining constant, will automatically decrease

   A   Disposable income

   B   Discretionary income

   C   Nominal income

   D   Real income

32 Which of the policies below would *not* be used to combat inflation?

   A   Subsidise production costs of domestic firms

   B   Appreciate the domestic currency

   C   Raising the minimum wage

   D   Raising labour productivity

33 Costs of unemployment do *not* include

   A   Falling output

   B   Falling inflation

   C   Falling aggregate demand

   D   Higher government spending

34 Costs of high inflation do *not* include

   A   Reduced purchasing power of consumers

   B   Uncertainty about the future

   C   Increasing costs of production for businesses

   D   Higher export prices for price inelastic products

35 One drawback of economic growth is

   A   Increased investment in the economy

   B   Increased employment

   C   Increased consumption expenditure

   D   Increased resource depletion

36 International trade quotas do *not*

   A   Reduce the volume of imports

   B   Raise the price of imports

   C   Encourage international trade and exchange

   D   Encourage demand for domestically produced products

37 A key difference between quotas and tariffs is that the latter method

   A   Is more effective in reducing demand

   B   Is seen as less aggressive as a means of protectionism

   C   Raises revenue for the domestic government

   D   Raises prices of imports for customers and businesses

38 A dip in the level of economic activity is known as a

   A   Decline

   B   Recession

   C   Slump

   D   Peak

39 Which of the following is *not* a deflationary government policy?

   A Increased taxation

   B Reduced public expenditure

   C Raising interest rates

   D Devalued exchange rate

40 A fall in the foreign exchange rate is unlikely to lead to

   A Higher import prices

   B Cheaper export prices

   C A deficit on the Balance of Payments

   D Falling demand for imports

Unit 1.6   Organizational Planning Tools

Task 1: Complete the missing words

A .... framework is a systematic management tool used to deal with problems, concerns or issues faced by a business so that rational and sound decisions are made. For example, force field analysis is used to deal with the issue of .... management. Most decision-making models will examine the various position and beliefs of its .... (such as shareholders, managers and employees).

Business decisions are not always made purely on facts and quantifiable reasoning. Instead, key decisions are often based on gut feelings, emotions, i..................... (or instinct) and whether managers are comfortable with their decision, irrespective of any potential financial gains. Nevertheless, in making decisions, managers tend to consider both the benefits (financial and non-financial) and the costs before taking any firm action. Decision making is also likely to be affected by various ....
..............., e.g. it is probable that autocratic managers make decisions in a different manner from democratic or laissez faire managers.

SWOT analysis is a planning and decision-making tool that can help management to reduce the .... involved in making decisions. SWOT analysis involves exploring the current position of a product, department or the whole organization in terms of .... and .... and to identify potential .... and .... It is also common to find a SWOT analysis within a .... plan.

Task 2: Match the terms

Use the list below to identify the key term from the given definitions:

- Business plan
- Cost–benefit analysis
- Decision-making framework
- Decision tree
- Operational decisions
- Pareto Principle

Key Term	Definition
	A decision-making tool that diagramatically shows the probable outcomes (in monetary terms) that might result from the various decisions that a business can pursue.
	A report or document that outlines the particular tactics and strategies to be employed to meet a particular aim or objective of an organization.
	Refers to the everyday and regularly scheduled decisions made by management.
	Refers to any formal and systematic process of dealing with business problems, concerns or issues so that managers can make the best decisions.
	Often known as the 80/20 rule, this theory states that 20% of the input in any process generates 80% of the output, e.g. 20% of the firm's products make up 80% of its sales revenues.
	A decision-making model that examines the financial costs and benefits of a decision. Generally, if the financial gains exceed the costs of the decision, then managers will go ahead (on quantitative grounds).

Task 3: Explain …

a   The sort of decisions that are made by the Board of Directors of a company

_____

_____

_____

_____

b   Whether a business plan guarantees success

_____

_____

_____

_____

c   Two reasons for producing a business plan

_____

_____

d   Whether the following factors are strengths, weaknesses, opportunities or threats:

   i   high gearing

_____

_____

   ii   high market share

_____

_____

   iii   reduced entry barriers to the industry

_____

_____

   iv   new overseas markets to enter

_____

_____

Task 4: Multiple choice

1   Financial backers will be interested in the relative strengths and weaknesses of a business proposal. This can be done through examining a firm's

   A   Research Proposal

   B   Executive Summary

   C   Business Plan

   D   Annual Report

2   Under what circumstance would scientific decision-making be appropriate?

   A   When time is of the essence

   B   When dealing with ethical issues

   C   When finance for detailed market research is available

   D   When past experience is sought

3 Critical decisions and long-term decisions that set the overall direction for a business are known as

   A Operational decisions

   B Tactical decisions

   C Strategic decisions

   D Premeditated decisions

4 Which of the following would *not* be considered as a *Strength* in a SWOT analysis?

   A A high staff retention rate

   B A high staff turnover rate

   C A healthy product portfolio

   D A wide and loyal customer base

5 Which of the following would be least likely to be considered as an *Opportunity* in a SWOT analysis?

   A Entering new overseas markets

   B A merger with a rival firm

   C High level of staff motivation

   D The development of new products

6 Which of the following would *not* be considered as a *Threat* in a SWOT analysis?

   A Lower entry barriers in the industry

   B Industrial action from the workforce

   C A takeover bid from another company

   D Lower interest rates in the economy

7 A business plan is unlikely to include which of the following?

   A Statement of aims and objectives

   B Competitor analysis

   C Pricing policy

   D Cash flow statement

8 Which of the following documents is most likely to be placed at the beginning of a business plan?

   A Executive summary

   B Research proposal

   C Appendices

   D Bibliography

9 A typical decision-making framework will help to address all of the following questions, except

   A How the business intends to achieve its objectives

   B Where a business wants to be

   C Why it is important to reach the firm's goals

   D Identifying the current position of the business

10 Elements of a business plan are least likely to include

   A Marketing research

   B Marketing strategy

   C Ratio analysis

   D Sources of finance

11 [HL Only]   Decision making that is based on a person's own experiences and feelings is known as
   A Intuitive decision-making
   B Scientific decision-making
   C Strategic decision-making
   D Tactical decision-making

12 [HL Only]   Which advantage does *not* apply to the use of decision trees?
   A They set out decision-making problems in a clear and logical manner
   B They are based on important intuitive and qualitative factors that affect decision making
   C They provide a quick and visual interpretation of the likely outcomes of decisions that need to be made
   D They force managers to assess the risks made in pursuing certain decisions

13 [HL Only]   Drawbacks of using decision trees do *not* include which statement below?
   A The probabilities are only estimates and the outcomes are therefore uncertain
   B They ignore intuitive decision-making
   C They ignore social factors and legal constraints in the decision-making process
   D They ignore the financial costs of investment decisions

14 [HL Only]   Which statement below does *not* apply to the Ishikawa fishbone model of decision making?
   A It looks at the causes and effects of a particular problem or issue
   B It is a visual tool used to identify the root cause of a problem or issue
   C It places a monetary value on key decisions
   D It can be a useful brainstorming tool

15 [HL Only]   External constraints on business planning and decision making include
   A The availability of finance
   B Exogenous shocks
   C Organizational culture
   D Human resources

Unit 1.7   Growth and Evolution

Task 1: Complete the missing words

Internal growth refers to increasing the size of a firm by using its own resources, such as ....
profit. It is also known as .... growth. External growth occurs when a firm expands by merging
with or .... another firm. This method is often known as .... growth.

Firms looking for quick growth and expansion will tend to adopt .... growth strategies, such as
purchasing a majority stake in another company. This strategy is known as a .... By contrast, a
.... is where two or more companies share the financial risks and rewards of a
business project. The firms jointly establish and own a new business.

One benefit of organizational growth is economies of scale. These are .... savings due to the large
scale of business operations, i.e. .... costs of production fall as the level of output increases. The
main types of economies include financial, managerial, ... (or commercial) and marketing.

The .... (or best) size for a business depends on its aims, the structure of its costs and the size of
the market.

Task 2: Vocabulary quiz

Identify the key terms from the clues given. *Hint*: the answers are in alphabetical order.

Key Term	Definition
	Often a hostile method of growth that involves buying a majority stake in another business in order to take control of the target business.
	A form of integration which occurs between firms in unrelated business operations.
	A growth strategy that involves payment of an initial fee and ongoing royalty payments in return for the use of another firm's name, logos, products and trademarks.
	Form of external growth that occurs when a business integrates with another firm in the same industry.
	Growth of firms through mergers and takeovers of other businesses.
	Refers to the amalgamation of firms as a growth strategy.
	An agreement between two companies to form a single legal entity with its new or revised Board of Directors.
	Similar to a merger, this form of growth involves two or more firms working together on a specific business venture. However, they form a legally binding contract without losing their individual corporate identities.

Task 3: Economies and diseconomies of scale

a   Explain why is it relatively easier to enter the restaurant industry than to enter the pharmaceutical
manufacturing industry.

_____

_____

b   Outline two causes of *external* diseconomies of scale.

_____

_____

Task 4: True or false?

		True / False
a	Economies of scale are the reduction in costs achieved through increased output.	
b	Organic growth comes from increased sales revenue and profits, the latter of which is invested back in the business.	
c	A conglomerate merger takes place between two firms that are in different lines of business.	
d	A demerger takes place when a firm splits into smaller firms or sells a number of of its subsidiaries.	
e	Expanding overseas is an example of diversification as a growth strategy.	
f	Growth through horizontal mergers or acquisitions does not represent any growth in the industry.	
g	Private limited companies cannot be taken over.	
h	A franchisee offers a franchise to a franchisor.	
i	Conglomerates tend to be large multinationals that operate in many countries.	

Task 5: Ansoff's Matrix

a   Ansoff's Matrix is a framework for devising growth strategies for a business.   True or False?

b   Market penetration is the least risky strategy for growth.   True or False?

c   The highest risk strategy for growth is called ……………..………..

d   Skimming as a pricing strategy is most likely to feature in which of Ansoff's growth strategies? …………… ……………

e   Risk-bearing economies of scale may be enjoyed if a business pursues which growth strategy? ………………

f   According to Ansoff, aiming to increase market share would be a feature of which growth strategy? …………… ………………

g   Innovation and new ideas are features of which strategy for achieving growth? …………… ………………

h   'Buy One, Get One Free' offers will help a business to increase its market share.   True or False?

i   Fill in the missing table below using the four growth strategies from Ansoff's Matrix.

j   Explain why it is difficult to penetrate a saturated market.

_____

_____

k   Explain why diversification carries huge risks as a growth strategy.

_____

_____

Task 6: Explain the difference between …

a   Franchisee and Franchisor

_____

_____

b   Management buy-in and Management buy-out

_____

_____

c   Acquisitions and mergers

_____

_____

Task 7: Multiple choice – Economies and diseconomies

1   Which of the following is _not_ a reason a firm may choose to demerge (break up)?

A To avoid falling profits in the business

B To focus on a smaller range of products and services

C To enjoy economies of scale

D To focus more specifically at a target market

2   Internal diseconomies of scale can be caused by

A The exercise of control by managers being weakened with a larger workforce

B Being unable to purchase stock at a discounted price

C Traffic congestion causing delays to delivery of important stock

D Advertising costs to a global audience

3   Technological economies of scale can only be feasible for a business if

A Banks lend money for business to purchase the highly expensive technology

B Capital equipment is capable of producing mass units of a product in a short time

C There is sufficient market demand for the product

D There is an economic boom

4   External economies of scale are cost savings available to the whole …………… as a result of its
……………

A Industry, location

B Business, location

C Market, size

D Business, size

5   Multinational corporations do *not* benefit from

   A   Increased market size

   B   Potential diseconomies of scale

   C   Local labour skills

   D   International competitiveness

6   Average costs can be lowered if a firm produces a range of related products rather than producing individual products. This is known as the benefits of

   A   Internal economies of scale

   B   Economies of scope

   C   Diversification

   D   Increasing returns to scale

7   If a firm increases its use of all factors of production but sees an increase in its average costs, it is a sign of

   A   Internal diseconomies of scale

   B   External returns to scale

   C   Diminishing marginal returns

   D   Decreasing returns to scale

8   External economies of scale can arise from

   A   Bulk purchases of raw materials, parts and components at favourable prices

   B   The introduction and use of advanced technology which doubles production but only adds 50% to costs of production

   C   Specialized back-up services available in a particular region

   D   Lower interest rates, thereby reducing the cost of borrowing to large companies

9   In 2006, the Walt Disney Company agreed to a US$7.4bn (£4.1bn) deal to buy Pixar. This is an example of a(n)

   A   Merger

   B   Collaboration

   C   Acquisition

   D   Horizontal integration

10   Which of the following is *not* a cause of internal diseconomies of scale?

   A   Poor communication between different departments

   B   Lack of staff morale and motivation

   C   Less control, direction and coordination of human resources

   D   Late deliveries due to congestion in busy locations

11   If a firm doubles all its factor inputs and finds that output increases by 50%, then the firm is said to have experienced

   A   Growth

   B   Economies of Scale

   C   Decreasing returns to scale

   D   Diminishing returns to scale

12 The Ansoff Matrix suggests four possible methods of growth. Which of these is *not* one of the growth options?

   A Market penetration

   B Mergers and acquisitions

   C Market development

   D Diversification

13 Which business is least likely to benefit from economies of scope?

   A Amazon.com (online retailer)

   B Thomas Cook (travel agency)

   C IBID Press (publishers)

   D Ferrari (luxury car manufacturer)

14 Which of the following is *not* a valid argument for pursuing growth as an objective?

   A To achieve economies of scale

   B To achieve a greater market share

   C To increase chances of survival

   D To minimize internal communication problems

15 Internal economies of scale are those that

   A Result from changes in production techniques

   B Increase due to the growth of the industry as a whole

   C Generate lowering unit costs

   D Reduce units costs in the short run

Task 8: Multiple choice – External and organic growth

1 Which one of the following is least likely to be an advantage of forming a joint venture?

   A They allow firms to enjoy some of the advantages of mergers without losing their identity

   B Joint ventures are not as expensive as takeovers or mergers

   C Most joint ventures are friendly

   D Profits from the venture can be shared equally

2 Which one of the following is *not* a benefit of forming a conglomerate?

   A Economies of scale

   B Focused marketing

   C Spreading risks

   D Market power

3 Which of the following would *not* be found in Porter's model for growth?

   A Lowest cost supplier within a mass market

   B Highly differentiated products within a mass market

   C Lowest cost supplier within a focused market segment

   D Lowest cost supplier with image for high quality

4 Which of the following does *not* appear in Ansoff's Matrix?

   A Market penetration

   B Product extension

   C Market development

   D Market extension

5 An advantage of diversification could include

   A Extra time and resources devoted to the new venture

   B Economies of scale that may be achieved

   C Finance to fund the expansion plans

   D A lack of expertise, such as knowledge of new markets

6 A disadvantage of diversification is

   A Spreading risks

   B Opportunity to increase customer base

   C Entering new markets

   D Better management control

7 Horizontal integration occurs when

   A A firm acquires or merges with another firm at different stages of production

   B A firm acquires or merges with another firm at the same stage of production

   C Two or more firms that are in direct competition merge

   D Two or more firms that are not in direct competition merge

8 Which of the following is *not* a constraint on the growth of firms?

   A Government controls

   B Finance

   C Size of the market

   D Opportunities

9 A business grows in size due to its own finance and retained profits. This process is known as

   A Organic growth

   B Horizontal growth

   C Acquisition

   D Conglomerate

10 A franchise is the

   A Person who buys the right to use the products, image or name of a company or individual

   B Right to trade using another firm's products, name and image

   C Use of external growth to enlarge a multinational corporation

   D Person or business selling the right for others to use their name, image or products

11 A merger between two newspaper companies is an example of

   A Vertical integration

   B Horizontal integration

   C Lateral amalgamation

   D Conglomerate merger

12 A merger occurs when two firms ……….. to form a new company to achieve benefits of
……………. growth.

    A Agree, corporate

    B Decide, external

    C Agree, external

    D Choose, organic

13 Organic growth cannot be achieved through

    A Increased sales turnover

    B Increased staff turnover

    C Increased capital expenditure (investment)

    D Increased prices for certain products

14 Which statement *cannot* be applied to internal growth?

    A It is financed through retained profits of a firm

    B It relies on the production and marketing of a firm's products

    C It is a relatively cheaper method of growth

    D It is suitable for firms looking to grow rapidly

15 Which statement below does *not* explain why small firms can survive and flourish?

    A Local monopoly power

    B Financial aid from the government for small businesses

    C Being able to provide a personalised service

    D Choice of finance options

16 The process by which two different organizations contribute resources to a shared project by
forming a separate enterprise is known as

    A External growth

    B A strategic alliance

    C A joint venture

    D Collaboration

17 The integration of two firms in completely different industries is known as

    A Inorganic growth

    B Diversification

    C Vertical integration

    D Horizontal integration

18 Which statement below does *not* apply to franchises?

    A The franchisee can buy or lease a franchise

    B Franchisors have little if any control over the way the franchise operates

    C A franchisor can expand its business without incurring huge debts

    D The failure rate is low since franchisees are generally very motivated

19 The low-risk growth option where firms operate in a known market with familiar products is known in Ansoff's Matrix as

  A Market Penetration

  B Market Growth

  C Market Orientation

  D Product development

20 One potential disadvantage of mergers is a change in

  A Access to technology and human resources

  B Synergy

  C Market power

  D Corporate culture

21 An advantage of a takeover bid to the buyer includes

  A Changes to corporate identity

  B Potential conflicts between the two businesses

  C Possible redundancies

  D Potential market dominance

22 Virgin Mobile is a business collaboration between the Virgin Group and Deutsche Telekom. Virgin Mobile is therefore an example of a

  A Franchise

  B Partnership

  C Joint venture

  D Subcontractor

23 Which statement below does *not* apply to franchising as a form of growth?

  A The franchisee owns the business once a contract is signed by both parties

  B Arrangement and administration fees and royalty payments must be paid to the franchisor

  C The franchisee can buy or lease the franchised business

  D Franchising is considered as a form of internal growth

24 McDonald's introduction of salads and alternative burgers has helped it to raise sales in existing markets. Which of Igor Ansoff's growth strategies does this describe?

  A Market penetration

  B Market development

  C Product development

  D Diversification

25 In Ansoff's Matrix, ………….. is the marketing of existing products in existing markets.

  A Market penetration

  B Market development

  C Market planning

  D Market growth

26 Multinationals that market their products by expanding to overseas markets is an example of

 A Diversification

 B Market development

 C Market penetration

 D Product development

27 Reasons for airlines to form a strategic alliance include all of the following except:

 A It allows the airline companies to keep their separate identities

 B It provides benefits from economies of scale from combined purchasing and marketing power

 C They can grow through diversification

 D They can cover more destinations by joining forces

28 Porter's generic strategy that focuses on being the lowest cost provider of a good or service in order to charge low prices yet remain profitable is called

 A Franchising

 B Cost leadership

 C Price leadership

 D Focus

29 The process of taking over another firm's brands rather than the whole company is known as

 A Brand acquisition

 B Brand buy out

 C Differentiation

 D Partial acquisition

30 In 2006, L'Oreal (the world's largest cosmetics and beauty firm) bought out The Body Shop. This is an example of

 A Merging

 B Management buy-out

 C Horizontal integration

 D Diversification

Unit 1.8 Change and the Management of Change [Higher Level Extension]

Task 1: Complete the missing words

Imposing change on the workforce may be demotivating and demoralizing due to the r.................. to change. Good change management may require managers to:

- Forecast and p........ for change in advance
- Be proactive in creating a change c.......... within the organization
- C.................. with staff to inform them of planned changes and to engage in a process of consultation
- Emphasize the p.............. effects of the proposed change to win support from the staff
- Provide support and counselling to those most negatively affected by change, such as those who may lose their jobs through r...................... or those who may be demoted
- Provide t................. as appropriate to help workers adapt to the proposed changes

Most theorists agree that effective change management usually requires some form of input from the employees. This can be done in several different ways such as through staff c.................... and participation. The success of any change process reflects the w.................... of the staff to adapt to the proposed changes. To minimize their misunderstanding and reluctance to adapt to change, employees should be somewhat involved in the change process.

Task 2: True or false?

		True / False
a	All change, no matter what size, has implications for staff.	
b	The management of people is the easiest part of change management.	
c	Knowledge of corporate culture is important to managing change.	
d	One of the advantages of force field analysis is that it helps managers to identify the stakeholders affected by a change.	
e	Leadership style directly affects the degree of success in managing change.	
f	Misunderstandings and miscommunication are sources of resistance to change.	
g	Kruger argues that 'opponents' have a pessimistic outlook towards change since they cannot see any personal benefits from such change.	
h	Senior management have a permanent task and challenge in managing change in their organizations.	

Task 3: Explain …

a Why a vision is important when introducing change

_____

_____

b Why managing a merger tends to be easier than managing a crisis

_____

_____

c   Two constraints to effective change management

i   _____

_____

ii   _____

_____

d   Why it may be important to consult staff in decision making

_____

_____

Task 4: Vocabulary quiz

Identify the key terms from the clues given. *Hint*: the answers are in alphabetical order.

Key Term	Definition
	A management response to a major and probably unpredicted threat to an organization, such as a fire or extremely bad press coverage.
	Forces acting for change.
	Lewin's model of change management (forces for and against change).
	Pressure from staff against change being introduced, i.e. a reluctance to change.

Task 5: Multiple choice

1   Initially, in dealing with restraining forces a business is most likely to

   A   Carry out a cost-benefit analysis

   B   Conduct a SWOT analysis

   C   Identify key impediments to change

   D   Communicate the purpose of change to its staff

2   Which of the following is unlikely to be an incentive to reduce resistance to change?

   A   Performance related pay

   B   Teamworking

   C   Promotional opportunities

   D   Autocratic leadership

3   Force field analysis is

   A   Not of any use to inward looking organizations

   B   Used to examine the reasons for change

   C   Subjective since weights can be skewed in favour of management preferences

   D   Useful for examining external factors affecting change

4   To overcome resistance to change, a business may choose to

   A   Adopt a dictatorial leadership style to implement change

   B   Communicate every stage of the change process via email to accelerate developments

   C   Hold a staff meeting to explain why the changes are necessary

   D   Entice staff to conform to change by promising future pay rises

5   Which of the following is unlikely to be a core feature, rather than an outcome, of effective change management?

    A Gaining the support for change from all staff members

    B Communicating the rationale for all changes to overcome resistance and fears

    C Summarizing the net benefits of change

    D Providing training opportunities to cope with and adapt to the change

6   Factors that push for change in an organization are known as

    A Driving forces

    B Restraining forces

    C Power forces

    D Motivating forces

7   Which factor is *not* a cause of resistance to change?

    A Communication issues

    B Adaptive cultures

    C Inadequate or inaccurate information

    D Insecurities and fear of the unknown

8   Which of Kotter's approaches to change management is a 'Theory X' manager most likely to adopt?

    A Education and communication

    B Facilitation and support

    C Manipulation and co-option

    D Explicit and implicit coercion

9   Which option does *not* suggest why the change process might fail?

    A Inert organizational cultures

    B Inability to communicate the vision for change

    C Not planning for short-term results

    D Empowerment of staff

10   The management of change is made difficult by a range of factors. Which factor below does *not* present a barrier to effective change management?

    A The fear of change, e.g. job losses or cuts in remuneration

    B Individuals unable to reach their higher level needs, e.g. recognition through promotion or self-actualization

    C Training needs (to adapt to the change) which might prove to be expensive and time consuming

    D Managers finding it difficult to change their management style to accommodate the change

Unit 1.9 Globalization

Task 1: Complete the missing words

Globalization refers to the growing degree of .... and interdependence of the world's economy. This means that decisions and actions taken in one part of the world will have a direct impact on those in other parts of the world.

A key contributing factor to globalization is the growth and expansion of ....
.... (MNC). There is increasing pressure for these global businesses to market their brands worldwide. .... progress, such as e-commerce, has also contributed to globalization by improving consumer access to a huge range of markets.

Globalization has both positive and detrimental effects on businesses. For example, it stimulates .... since there are more foreign firms and products competing in the domestic market. At the same time, the .... of trade restrictions has allowed domestic businesses to enter overseas markets, thereby enabling these firms to benefit from .... (lower average costs as a firm expands its operations) and a larger .... base. However, with more competition comes greater consumer sovereignty, i.e. the consumer has greater choice and can be more selective about price, quality and customer care.

Task 2: Explain two ...

a   Effects of globalization on business activity

  _____

  _____

b   Reasons why joining a regional trading bloc might lead to more unemployment in the short run

  _____

  _____

  _____

  _____

c   Reasons why knowledge of business etiquette might be important to firms planning to expand overseas

  _____

  _____

  _____

  _____

d   Ways in which technological developments have led to globalization

  _____

  _____

  _____

  _____

e   Ways in which multinational corporations have led to globalization

_____

_____

_____

_____

f   Benefits for a multinational corporation that operates within a regional trading bloc

_____

_____

_____

_____

g   Potential drawbacks of overseas expansion for a multinational company

_____

_____

_____

_____

Task 3: True or false?

		True / False
a	The sales revenue of large multinationals often far exceeds the GDP of many countries.	
b	Globalization can be defined as an increase in international trade across the world.	
c	Multinational companies are public limited companies that operate overseas.	
d	Cultural exports have led to increased globalization.	
e	A regional trading bloc allows member countries from all over the world to unite to remove barriers to international trade.	
f	Trade liberalization has been a key driver of globalization.	
g	Quotas are a form of international protectionism.	
h	Multinationals can minimize their tax bills by operating in overseas countries.	

Task 4: Multiple choice

1   Firms that establish themselves overseas before any other competitor is able to do so are likely to enjoy the exclusive benefit of

  A Economies of scope

  B Economies of scale

  C First mover advantage

  D Brand loyalty

2   Members of a free trade area agree to remove all the following except

  A Tariffs

  B Quotas

  C Taxes

  D Export restraints

3   Potential problems of overseas expansion do *not* include

   A Lack of local knowledge

   B Higher distribution costs

   C Language and cultural barriers

   D Lower tax liabilities

4   An advantage of *not* joining a trading bloc is the opportunity to

   A Exploit new market opportunities

   B Lower costs by operating in overseas markets

   C Enjoy economic independence

   D Spread risks

5   Which of the following is a drawback to a multinational expanding overseas?

   A The spreading of risks by not relying on any single economy

   B Opportunities for economies of scale

   C Different business etiquette and customs

   D Wage rates in less economically developed countries

6   Which one of the following reasons does *not* explain why multinationals are better than domestic rivals in the provision of goods and services?

   A Well-known brand names

   B Economies of scale in production, distribution and marketing

   C Better knowledge of local cultures

   D The economic power to influence or encourage national governments

7   Costs of globalization to a business do *not* include

   A Increased rivalry in the marketplace

   B Larger budget devoted to research and development

   C Relocation costs

   D Increasing returns to scale

8   Which option is *not* a potential problem for Chinese firm Lau & Chen Manufacturers expanding to the USA?

   A Differences in culture and language

   B Administration procedures and costs

   C Lack of infrastructure networks

   D Political conflict and restrictions

9   Globalization presents many opportunities for businesses. Which one of the options below is the most likely exception to this rule?

   A Mergers, acquisitions and joint ventures

   B Economies of scale

   C Larger customer base

   D Language translation

10 A free trade .... requires state members to remove trade .... with each other.

   A Area, barriers

   B Agreement, barriers

   C Area, conflict

   D Agreement, conflict

11 Which of the following is a disadvantage of joining a regional trading bloc?

   A Removal of barriers to trade

   B Promotes international trade of goods and services

   C Trade diversion

   D Trade creation

12 Reasons for a business developing overseas include

   A Incurring more risks

   B Favourable trading conditions in the domestic economy

   C Cheaper access to factors of production

   D Relocation costs

13 Which of the following is *not* a drawback of joining a regional trading bloc?

   A Unemployment could be created as domestic firms face increased competition

   B Trade diversion is created

   C Trade creation takes place

   D Policies taken by the RTB might not suit all member states

14 A valid argument for multinational firms in spending money on foreign direct investment is that

   A Businesses will make more money by operating overseas

   B It is a form of altruism

   C It can avoid trade restrictions

   D They benefit from economies of scope

15 All the statements below are valid arguments for limiting free international trade except

   A Opportunities for specialization

   B The protection of infant industries from international rivals

   C Political and strategic reasons

   D Protect domestic employment

16 Which of the following is least likely to be a barrier to international trading?

   A International business etiquette

   B Political and economic conflict

   C Cultural differences

   D Communication across geographical locations

17 Member countries of a trade agreement that agree to establishing a common external tariff to non-member states are collectively known as a

   A Customs union

   B Economic trading bloc

   C Partnership Agreement

   D Free trade area

18 The concept of adjusting global marketing techniques to better suit the varying needs of overseas customers is known as

   A Direct marketing

   B Glocalization

   C International marketing

   D Technology transfer

19 Barriers to globalization in developing countries do *not* include

    A Infrastructure

    B Distribution networks

    C Legal restrictions

    D Large populations

20 Benefits of globalization to a business include

    A Economies of scale

    B Rivalry

    C Price transparency

    D Increased market choice

HUMAN RESOURCES

UNIT

2

Unit 2.1   Human Resource Planning

Task 1: True or false?

		True / False
a	Induction training is intended for new employees to make acquaintance with the organization and key personnel.	
b	One benefit of training and development is lower levels of staff retention.	
c	Grievance can occur when there is conflict in the workplace.	
d	Employees can be instantly dismissed for breaking company policy, such as turning up to work in the wrong uniform.	
e	The main method of selection is via interview.	
f	Dismissal is fair if an employee is asked to leave due to incompetence or major misconduct.	
g	The document that gives the profile of the ideal candidate for a job is called the job description.	
h	A zero rate of staff turnover is desirable.	
i	If a woman was offered less pay than a man for doing the same job, assuming they are of equal rank, then that would be illegal under equal opportunity laws.	

Task 2: Vocabulary quiz

Identify the key terms from the clues given. *Hint*: the answers are in alphabetical order.

a   **[HL Only]**   Employment rights and legislation

Key Term	Definition
	Law that requires employers to treat disabled persons equally as others, unless there are justified reasons for positive discrimination.
	Legislation that requires employers to treat both sexes equally in terms of pay and other conditions of employment, assuming they have the same qualities (e.g. education, skills and experience).
	Laws imposed to ensure that the wellbeing (including the physical protection) of workers is not affected by their work.
	Ruling against negative discrimination on the grounds of race, ethnicity, colour or nationality in terms of employment.
	Law that makes discrimination on the grounds of sex or marital status illegal in all aspects of employment (e.g. recruitment and promotion).
	European Union legislation that sets a limit (48 hours) on maximum number of hours that employees need to work in a week. Employees who are asked to and also choose to work beyond the limit must be paid overtime.

b Human resource management

Key Term	Definition
	The number of people away from work as a percentage of the size of the workforce in a business, per period of time.
	The study of what is included in a job, such as the tasks, responsibilities and skills involved.
	Measures the rate of change of human resources within an organization, per period of time.
	A document detailing the required skills, qualifications and experience of the ideal candidate for a job.
	Measures the output of workers; often expressed as the output per worker.
	Relocating or reposting a worker to another part of a business as there is no longer a need for the current position.
[HL Only]	Charles Handy's theory that organizations face constant change (and hence need to be able to adapt accordingly), and that the changing organization is comprised of three 'leafs' of workers: core workers, insourced workers and outsourced workers.

c Training, appraisal and dismissal

Key Term	Definition
	Process of collecting information and evidence to assess the performance of an employee.
	The termination of a person's employment contract because of unsatisfactory work performance, a breach of contract or gross misconduct at work.
	Training provided for new employees to introduce them to the premises, their new colleagues and their new job roles.
	A form of training that happens whilst the trainee is actually doing the job.

Task 3: The legal rights of employees [Higher Level Extension]

a Complete the missing words from the statements below.

i Dismissal is regarded as being …………… if a worker is made to leave a job for reasons other than a lack of competence or if they have not …………… their contract.

ii During a recession or poor trading periods, it may be necessary for a business to downsize its workforce by introducing voluntary or involuntary ……..……………

iii Termination of employment contracts can happen due to ……………… (when workers leave the workforce due to their age) and …………………… (when employees choose to leave their jobs).

iv Employees who have a case of unfair dismissal can take matters to an …………… tribunal.

v Theft or deliberate damage to company property can lead to instant dismissal on the grounds of gross misconduct. True or False?

vi Employers who own their own business have the right to hire and fire people without giving a reason.   True or False?

vii It is legal for an employer to dishonour the period of notice given to an employee as stated on their employment contract if the employee reveals trade secrets to rival firms.   True or False?

b Study the job advertisement below. Rewrite the advertisement so that it will attract the right type of candidate without breaching employment legislation.

> K&Q Gadgets Manufacturers Ltd.
> Require two female workers:
> Receptionist and Sales Assistant
> Must be:
> Attractive in appearance, tall, hardworking, intelligent
> American-origin, aged 18–25.
> Qualifications:
> IB Diploma or above
> Tel: John on (852) 2659 1825
> for more details or visit KQGML.com

_____

_____

_____

_____

_____

_____

_____

_____

_____

_____

_____

_____

c Which option below cannot be used to fairly dismiss a worker?

i Discriminatory behaviour

ii Harassment

iii Sleeping on the job

iv Grievance

d If a worker decides to leave their current employer for another organization, then this is classed as

i Retrenchment

ii Retirement

iii Resignation

iv Fair dismissal

e Gross misconduct in the workplace does *not* include

i Embezzlement

ii Incompetence

iii Drunk and disorderly behaviour

iv Violent behaviour

f   Changing an employee's terms and conditions of employment such as their working hours or their location of work so that s/he leaves the organization is considered as

   i   Discrimination

   ii   Retrenchment

   iii   Constructive dismissal

   iv   Ad hoc dismissal

g   The difference between retrenchment and dismissal is that

   i   Dismissals are voluntary

   ii   Retrenchments are voluntary

   iii   Retrenchments occur due to no fault of the employee

   iv   Dismissals come with compensation packages

h   Which Act covers issues relating to gender, age, religion, ethnic background, marital status and race in the workplace?

   i   Equal opportunities legislation

   ii   Anti-discrimination legislation

   iii   Equal pay legislation

   iv   Grievance legislation

i   Work out the total compensation that a sales executive can claim from the employer if a case of unfair dismissal is proved after three months of being dismissed. All figures are per month.

   • Wages: $3,000

   • Sales commission: 5%

   • Pension payments: $100

   • Education allowance: $200

   • Housing allowance: $250

   • Sales revenue: $25,000

j   The UK introduced its national minimum wage in 1999, setting the hourly figure at £3.60 for those aged over 21. By 2007, this figure had risen to £5.52. Calculate the percentage increase in costs for a UK-based business, assuming no other changes in its cost structure.

Task 4: Explain ...

a   Why it is important to set a deadline date on job advertisements

b   What is meant by an 'appraisal interview'

c   Why training and development are important to a business

_____

_____

_____

_____

d   Why training and development are important for employees

_____

_____

_____

_____

e   Whether an appraisal should be linked to pay

_____

_____

f   Advantages of internal promotion of employees

_____

_____

g   Two advantages to a business in using external recruitment

_____

_____

_____

_____

h   The difference between psychometric tests and aptitude tests

_____

_____

i   Two advantages of on-the-job training

_____

_____

_____

_____

j   Two disadvantages of on-the-job training

_____

_____

_____

_____

k Two advantages of internal recruitment

_____

_____

_____

_____

l Two benefits of low staff turnover

_____

_____

_____

_____

Task 5: High or low?

Explain whether the following measures of personnel effectiveness should, ideally, be high or low.

a Absenteeism

_____

_____

b Staff turnover

_____

_____

c Productivity

_____

_____

d Wastage

_____

_____

e Staff retention

_____

_____

Task 6: Multiple choice – Workforce planning

1 Which of the following is *not* a task of human resource planning?
   A Recruitment
   B Retention
   C Discipline and Dismissal
   D Payment of wages and salaries

2 The ability of a business to keep its employees working for the firm, rather than to seek employment elsewhere is known as
   A Internal recruitment
   B Retention
   C Selection
   D Presenteeism

3 Which option below will *not* necessarily reduce the supply of labour within an organization?

   A Redeployment

   B Retirement

   C Competition

   D Government legislation

4 The inability of a worker to switch from one job to another due to a lack of expertise or qualifications is known as

   A Occupational immobility

   B Geographical immobility

   C Structural unemployment

   D Labour immobility

5 Advantages of working from home do *not* include

   A Time and money saved by not having to travel

   B Personal life and work–life balance

   C Autonomy in decision making

   D Tax allowances for using personal property for business

6 A teleworker can benefit most from

   A Distractions by and interactions with family members

   B The absence of company policy such as dress code

   C Working in isolation every day

   D Costs of electricity being shared by the employer

7 Which of the following is *not* an effect of an ageing working population?

   A Lower levels of labour productivity

   B A decline in the dependent population

   C Changing patterns of employment and consumption

   D Reduced labour mobility

8 The supply of labour for a business is least directly affected by

   A Training and development programmes offered by the business

   B The dynamics of the internal workforce

   C An ageing population

   D An increase in examination standards set by the industry

9 If the workforce of Gifford and Leung Ltd is 85 people and twelve of them resign this year, then the staff turnover rate at the company is

   A 7%

   B 14%

   C 12 people

   D 73 people

10 Which of the following is likely to be a cause of high labour turnover for a business?

   A Attractive salaries and fringe benefits

   B Investment in training and development

   C High occupational mobility of the workforce

   D High staff morale

11 Which of the following is *not* a trend in the labour market?

  A More people are taking up part-time jobs

  B More women are joining the workforce

  C More people are self-employed

  D More people are working at the office rather than from home

12 Natural wastage is the term used to describe

  A Human errors in the production process

  B Faulty or substandard output that needs to be rectified

  C People or their job position that are not replaced when they leave the firm

  D Unused labour due to off-peak trading periods or an economic recession

13 Human Resources Management does *not* tend to deal with

  A Product design and development

  B Financial budgeting

  C Recruitment and selection

  D Performance appraisals

14 A job vacancy may arise due to

  A Zero staff turnover

  B Internal promotion of a worker

  C Decrease in sales

  D Technological advances and automation

15 Recent changes faced by Human Resources Managers do *not* include

  A Increase in part-time employment

  B Increases in the number of females seeking employment

  C An ageing population

  D Less focus on flexible working hours

16 A workforce plan will determine what .... exist in an organization and include a relevant job .... and person .... for each vacant position.

  A Vacancies, description, specification

  B Vacancies, specification, description

  C Jobs, outline, statement

  D Jobs, description, statement

17 Which of the following does *not* represent flexible working practices?

  A Part-time employment

  B Teleworking

  C Homeworking

  D Teamworking

18 A business that has a relatively high staff turnover rate faces a problem of ....

  A Recruitment

  B Selection

  C Retention

  D Motivation

19 Workforce planning is *not* concerned with

    A Recruitment and selection

    B Redeployment of staff

    C Staff redundancies and retrenchment

    D Organizational structure of the workforce

20 A post holder's existing job description and person specification are *not* used for

    A Identifying training needs

    B Job evaluation

    C Appraisals

    D Promoting employees

21 Interviews conducted by a group of interviewers all at the same time are known as

    A Mirror interviews

    B Sequence interviews

    C Panel interviews

    D Face to face interviews

22 A .... specializes in a particular field or industry, has a large database of potential applicants, and takes responsibility for the advertising and interviewing of posts. In return they charge a fee for their services.

    A Careers centre

    B Job centre

    C Recruitment agency

    D Headhunter

23 Which statement applies to flexitime workers?

    A They must work a minimum number of hours as required by their employer

    B They are in part-time employment

    C Flexitime workers choose to work, rather than the employer, whenever it suits them

    D They are employed in a number of different jobs, carried out simultaneously

24 What is used to measure the proportion of an organization's workforce that leaves during the course of a year?

    A Retirement age

    B Retention rate

    C Turnover rate

    D Absenteeism rate

25 Benefits of working from home for the teleworker include those listed below except

    A Avoiding the need to commute

    B Flexible working hours

    C Saving on rental or mortgage expenses

    D Improved work output, assuming discipline is maintained

Task 7: Multiple choice – Recruitment and selection

1   A person specification

    A   Looks at the essential skills and knowledge required to carry out a specific job role

    B   Identifies the personal achievements and employment history of a candidate

    C   Specifies the requirements of what the ideal person needs to do in the job

    D   Lists the responsibilities of the post holder

2   A job description for an Economics teacher is unlikely to include

    A   The additional duties of the teacher

    B   The job title

    C   The required level of teaching experience

    D   Description of role in relation to others in the organization

3   A person specification is unlikely to include the ………….. required from the ideal candidate.

    A   Skills

    B   Aptitude

    C   Responsibilities

    D   Experience

4   Which option is *not* a reason for rejecting candidates based on their application form for a job?

    A   A mismatch of skills and qualifications

    B   Insufficient work experience

    C   Low score in aptitude assessment

    D   Employer has set a limit on number of candidates to shortlist

5   Which of the following does *not* explain why businesses need to recruit workers?

    A   Business is expanding due to increasing demand for its products

    B   Existing employees leave the firm due to retirement

    C   To avoid diseconomies of scale

    D   To cover maternity and paternity leave

6   Which of the following would *not* appear in a job description?

    A   Job Title

    B   Main tasks and accountabilities

    C   Skills and qualifications

    D   Responsibilities

7   The length and type of induction training depend(s) on:

    i   the size of the business

    ii   the rank or position held by the employee

    iii   the complexity of the job

    A   i and ii only

    B   ii and iii only

    C   i and iii

    D   All of them

8 In an interview, a question such as, "What would you do if you saw a fellow worker stealing?" is an example of what type of question?

   A Risk assessment questions

   B Situational based questions

   C Behavioural based questions

   D Aptitude questions

9 Interviews do *not* allow an employer to find out further information about an applicant such as

   A Their ability to converse and articulate an argument

   B Details about their work history

   C Ability to perform certain tasks

   D The level of enthusiasm shown by the applicant

10 Using an existing worker to fill a vacancy of a senior position solves the problem of having to

   A Train the new worker in the job

   B Find a suitable employee to fill the vacancy

   C Assess the suitability of a candidate to fit into the culture of the organization

   D Advertise the job to suitable candidates

11 Which of the following is *not* a feature of flexible working patterns?

   A More employment of part-time and peripheral staff

   B More mobile workers

   C Taller hierarchical structures

   D Greater numbers of people working from home

12 Potential disadvantages to a business of high labour turnover do *not* include

   A Lost production during recruitment, induction and training

   B The wages needed to pay new staff

   C The cost of recruitment and selection

   D Lack of continuity or expertise

13 Which of the following is *not* a disadvantage of interviews as a form of recruitment?

   A They do not reveal truly whether an applicant can do the job

   B Detailed questions can be asked

   C Information given might be biased

   D Might put pressure on applicants

14 The document that acts as a final safety check to confirm all information given by an applicant is correct is known as the

   A Curriculum Vitae

   B Proforma

   C Personal Statement

   D Reference

15 Which of the following is least likely to appear in a person specification for a person working in new product design?

    A Innovative

    B Creative

    C Team player

    D Skilled in customer relations

16 Which of the following is *not* classed as dismissal?

    A Redundancy

    B Gross misconduct

    C Being 'fired' or 'sacked'

    D Suspension

17 Objectives of recruitment advertising do *not* include

    A Informing potential candidates about job opportunities

    B Providing information about the firm to possible applicants

    C Dissuading unsuitable applicants

    D Attracting as many applicants as possible to apply for the job

18 Which statement below always applies to recruitment advertisements?

    A They can be published internally and externally

    B They publish the salary and benefits in order to attract applicants

    C They state the requirement of a curriculum vitae from applicants

    D They show the company website for those interested in finding out more information

19 The document that outlines the work history and achievements of a job applicant is known as the

    A Application form

    B Curriculum Vitae

    C Job Description

    D Job Appraisal

20 Top Tutors Ltd. specializes in finding part-time and temporary work for teachers by matching the requirements of students who seek private tuition lessons. The business is therefore an example of a ....

    A Consultancy firm

    B Recruitment agency

    C Head hunter

    D Job centre

21 The advertising of an internal position is most likely to be in the form of

    A A newspaper announcement

    B A television advertisement

    C An Internet advertisement

    D A staff bulletin notice

22 In order to test or assess the ability of a candidate to handle their job, recruiters can use

    A Assessment testing

    B Panel interviews

    C Psychometric testing

    D Aptitude testing

23 .... tests can be used to assess the .... of candidates, such as their level of motivation or their ability to handle stressful situations.

    A Aptitude, attitude

    B Psychometric, attitude

    C Aptitude, ability

    D Attitude, ability

24 A benefit of high staff retention is that

    A Recruitment and induction costs are reduced

    B New people and ideas come into the business

    C Staffing costs are lowered

    D There is minimal continuity and stability

25 A drawback of using internal recruitment is

    A A lack of 'new blood' in the business

    B Reduces 'dead wood' in the organization

    C The relative cost of recruitment

    D The relative amount of time needed for recruitment

Task 8: Multiple choice – Training, development and appraisals

1 Which option below would *not* be a feature of an induction programme?

    A Learning about the responsibilities in the job

    B Meeting subordinates, line manager and new colleagues

    C Having a tour of the premises

    D An appraisal meeting

2 Which of the following is least likely to be classed as a method of on-the-job training?

    A Demonstrations to show trainees how to do a job

    B Coaching and mentoring between an experienced employee and the trainee

    C Attending specialist conferences

    D Job rotation within the workplace

3 Which of the following is *not* a method of off-the-job training?

    A Employees attend a training centre

    B Work shadowing

    C Evening classes

    D Self-study / Distance learning

4   Induction training is unlikely to cover

    A   The basics of the worker's job

    B   The history of the business

    C   Facts and figures of the business, e.g. number of employees

    D   Upgrading of ICT skills needed for the job

5   Which of the following is *not* an aim of training and development?

    A   Match the skills of people to the needs of the organization

    B   Improve the quality of people's work

    C   Improve customer service and relations

    D   Gain higher budget allocated to the HRM Department

6   Appraisals that involve gathering information concerning the appraisee from different groups of people who work with the employee are known as

    A   360 degree appraisals

    B   Stakeholder appraisals

    C   Peer appraisals

    D   Upwards appraisals

7   Off-the-job training refers to training that is

    A   Conducted at the place of work whilst the employee is not working

    B   Conducted by specialist trainers not necessarily available at the workplace

    C   Carried out for newly appointed staff

    D   Funded by the government or training colleges

8   Which of the following training courses would be classed as personal, rather than professional, training and development for a teacher of IB Business & Management?

    A   First-aid course

    B   Teaching and learning strategies

    C   Raising standards in the Internal Assessment

    D   Teaching TOK in Business & Management

9   One problem with appraisal methods that use rating scales is that

    A   They are relatively expensive to conduct compared to other appraisal methods

    B   They lack structure in design

    C   Some traits that are scaled may not be directly relevant to job performance

    D   They are not standardized so makes comparisons very difficult

10   Which of the given appraisal method is most structured?

    A   360 degree

    B   Peer

    C   Essay

    D   Rating

Unit 2.2 Organizational Structure

Task 1: Complete the missing words

The 'span of control' refers to the .... of staff that a person is responsible for. For example, the Head of a large department will have a .... span of control. A manager with a narrow span of control means that he or she is responsible for relatively fewer people. There has been much debate about the .... (or best) size for a manager's direct span of control. There is no consensus on this as there are advantages and disadvantages to both options.

A .... hierarchical structure tends to give more responsibility to workers and can therefore lead to a higher level of motivation. .... occurs when a line manager passes on authority to others to perform a role or task. The line manager retains overall responsibility but the work is carried out by empowered subordinates.

By contrast, a .... organizational structure offers greater opportunities for promotion, closer management and supervision, ... chains of command and a .... span of control.

Task 2: Explain two reasons why ...

a Many firms are downsizing and delayering

_____

_____

_____

_____

b Effective delegation may help to motivate workers

_____

_____

_____

_____

c A matrix structure might cause problems for a business

_____

_____

_____

_____

d It is important for businesses to understand their informal structures

_____

_____

_____

_____

Task 3: Crossword – Organizational structure

Clues Across

4 The official path that instructions are passed on
7 Management guru who argues for flatter structures
8 Such structures help to improve communication
9 Personnel organized into a group
10 Holding someone responsible for their actions
13 The size (number) of the firm's employees
16 The act of passing down responsibility to others
19 The yearly meeting held for all key stakeholders
20 Person who inspires their team and staff
22 A sense of duty for others in your team

Clues Down

1 The person directly above you in the organization
2 Structure with many levels in the hierarchy
3 Long-term goal, often expressed as a statement
5 The top person in a company
6 Removing layers in the hierarchy to cut costs
11 Teams formed naturally, through unofficial means
12 The levels or ranks in an organization chart
14 Person with authority and responsibility for staff
15 Span of control that encompasses many people
17 Flexible organizational structure for projects
18 A particular job that needs to be done
21 Type of authority over those directly below you

Task 4: True or false?

		True / False
a	A flat organization has few layers of management.	
b	The span of control is inversely related to the number of layers in an organization.	
c	A wide span of control requires effective delegation of authority and responsibility.	
d	Delegation comes with extra financial rewards, e.g. pay rises.	
e	Responsibility cannot be delegated, i.e. it always remains the authority of the line manager.	
f	Authority cannot be delegated to subordinates.	
g	A key drawback of tall hierarchical structures is the potential for miscommunication problems due to the large number of layers in the organization.	
h	Line managers have a wide span of control in tall hierarchical structures.	
i	A driving force for delayering is to improve communication flows.	

Task 5: Distinguish between ...

    a   Accountability and responsibility

          _____

          _____

    b   The role of directors and the role of managers

          _____

          _____

    c   Hierarchical and flat structures

          _____

          _____

Task 6: Multiple choice

    1   Groups that are *not* an official part of an organization but arise from people having similar interests are known as

        A Specialist interest groups

        B Lobbying groups

        C Informal groups

        D Friendship groups

    2   Which of the options below is the most likely benefit of delayering to a business?

        A Wider spans of control

        B Increased delegation to subordinates

        C Shorter chains of command

        D Improved motivation

3 The person at the top of a hierarchy is known as the

    A Executive Director

    B Non-executive Director

    C Managing Director

    D Governing Director

4 Which option is an advantage of a wide span of control?

    A Communication is enhanced as there are more managers

    B It is more cost effective due to less hierarchical levels

    C Workers become more motivated as there are promotional prospects

    D Managers are freed to deal with other tasks

5 Decentralisation means

    A Orders are sent from the senior management team as they need to oversee corporate strategy

    B Passing responsibility and authority away from the senior management team to individual departments

    C Removing decision making power from managers

    D Informal communication between staff from various departments

6 Who is a senior manager directly accountable to?

    A Directors

    B Chief Executive

    C Supervisors

    D Shareholders

7 As a business grows, managers will need to relinquish some of their roles and responsibilities. This is known as

    A Delegation

    B Empowerment

    C Entrustment

    D Laissez-faire

8 Advantages of matrix systems do *not* include

    A Flexibility

    B Cross functional teamworking

    C Decentralized decision making

    D Improved control

9 Which of the following is a drawback of using matrix organizational structures?

    A Taller hierarchical structures

    B Narrower spans of control

    C Conflicting interest from having more than one line manager

    D Reduced employee empowerment

10 Which type of organizational structure is based on personal relationships and social networks?

    A Matrix

    B Hierarchical

    C Informal

    D Centralized

11 Drawbacks of informal organizational structures do *not* include

    A The spreading of rumours

    B Reduced bureaucracy

    C Misinterpretation of the correct information

    D Confidential information being exposed

12 Which term is used to describe the act of transferring a business function or activity to an organization operating overseas?

    A Decentralization

    B Offshoring

    C Outsourcing

    D Globalization

13 Which term is used to describe the system of organizing people within a business by rank?

    A Hierarchy

    B Span of control

    C Chain of command

    D Delegation

14 Which type of flexible organizational structure is based on different departments temporarily working together to achieve an organizational objective?

    A Decentralized

    B Outsourcing

    C Matrix management

    D Shamrock organization

15 Which of the following features applies to organizations with flat structures?

    A A large number of managers

    B Suitable when employees are multi-skilled

    C Good opportunities for promotion of staff

    D Narrow spans of control

Unit 2.3   Communication

Task 1: True or false?

		True / False
a	Communication can be simply defined as the flow of information from one person to another.	
b	Noise is a cause of communication failure.	
c	A memorandum is used for passing on messages to external agencies and firms.	
d	A pie chart is used to present time-series data.	
e	Grapevine communication refers to informal communication, such as gossip, within an organization.	
f	Letters can be used for internal communications.	

Task 2: Explain ...

a   Which of the following is *not* a form of non-verbal communication
  - Memorandums
  - Notices
  - Meetings
  - Reports

b   Why visual aids might be used during a presentation

c   The odd one out: email, letters, bulletin, fax, telephone, or video-conferencing

d   The best method of communication for sending weekly sales data to the regional director

Task 3: Outline two ...

a   Barriers to effective communication

b   Methods of written communication, other than letters

c Visual methods of communication, other than posters

_____

_____

d Benefits of information technology as a means of communication

_____

_____

Task 4: Correct categories

Place the following communication methods into the correct category in the table below. Then identify whether the method is used as internal, external or both.

Communication method	Internal	External
Written:		
Verbal:		
Informal:		
Information Communication Technology:		

- Appraisals
- Department meetings
- Email
- Faxes
- Feedback
- Grapevine
- Internet
- Memorandum
- Posters
- Presentations
- Report
- Telephones

Task 5: Vocabulary quiz

Identify the key terms from the clues given. *Hint*: the answers are in alphabetical order.

Key Term	Definition
	The vertical transfer of data from line manager to subordinates via a series of meetings.
	A method of improving communication by reducing the levels in an organizational hierarchy.
	A form of communication that occurs when people talk to each other in person.
	Using communication channels that are established by a business organization.
	A written record of the issues discussed in a business meeting.
	This causes communication breakdown, e.g. jargon, ignorance or computer failure.
	Communication via the use of spoken words, e.g. meetings and telephone conversations.

Task 6: Match the terms

Match the paper-based method of communication below that is best suited for the stated task.

	Communication Method				Purpose
A	Agenda			V	To remind staff of opportunities for training courses
B	Letter			W	To respond to a customer complaint
C	Memorandum			X	To inform staff of the issues to be discussed in a meeting
D	Notice			Y	To gain feedback from receiver and sender
E	Two way			Z	To inform a manager of a change in an appointment time

Task 7: Multiple choice

1 Which one of the following is *not* an objective of internal communication?

   A To provide information such as sales revenue figures

   B To give instructions such as how to operate machinery

   C To encourage more trade with customers

   D To give feedback such as appraisal interviews

2 Which one of the following is least likely to be an objective of external communication?

   A To provide information such as profit or loss figures

   B To receive feedback such as consumers' perceptions of a restaurant

   C To confirm orders by a specified time

   D To inform staff of a changed venue for a meeting

3 Which of the following is *not* a disadvantage of using information technology for communication?

   A Training costs

   B Expense of buying equipment

   C Records being backed up

   D Security issues, such as hackers

4 Identify the option from the list below that does *not* refer to verbal communication

   A Business meetings

   B Bulletin

   C Grapevine

   D Cascading

5 Identify the option that is *not* an example of formal communication

   A Departmental meetings

   B Trade union meetings

   C Staff appraisal

   D Grapevine communication

6 Informal communication could include all but

   A Spreading rumours

   B Emails to a supplier

   C Staff discussion during break times

   D Social outings

7 Which option is *not* a likely cause of communication failure?

   A Language and cultural awareness

   B Lack of interest in the message from the recipient, such as junk mail

   C Tall hierarchy within the organization

   D Geographical distance for global firms

8 Which of the following statements about internal communication is false?

   A Occurs between employees of a business

   B Helps to ensure that employees work towards a common goal

   C Requires feedback from recipients

   D Can be used to communicate to all members of the workforce

9 Which of the following is *not* an example of external communication?

   A Above-the-line promotion

   B Below-the-line promotion

   C Minutes of a meeting

   D Press releases

10 Effective communication can help to motivate the workforce, except for which reason below?

   A It requires time and planning from senior management

   B It gives direction and purpose to the employees

   C It gives employees opportunities to offer feedback and to give suggestions

   D It recognises achievements of employees and hence helps to reward them accordingly

11 Methods of obtaining feedback include the following, except
 A Telephone conversation
 B Face-to-face communication
 C Informal communication
 D Bulletin announcement

12 The chain of command refers to
 A The direct relationship between a superior and subordinates
 B The unofficial relationship between a superior and subordinates
 C The stages of production from primary to tertiary output
 D The instructions from a managing director

13 Communication that takes place outside of the business with individuals or organizations is called
 A Two-way communication
 B External communication
 C Formal communication
 D Oral communication

14 The document that notifies attendees of a business meeting of the topics to be discussed is called the
 A Agenda
 B Minutes
 C Bulletin
 D Memorandum

15 The transfer of information from one party to another is known as
 A Communication
 B Communication channels
 C Communication paths
 D Transmission mechanism

16 What are open channels of communication?
 A Gossip in the workplace
 B Formal communication that is transferred from one person to another
 C Sharing access to non-confidential information
 D Networking to get to meet business people and clients

17 What is meant by a restricted channel of communication?
 A When receivers have to pay for confidential and classified information
 B When information is confined to those who need to know
 C When only one channel of communication is used to pass on messages
 D When feedback is not required in communication

18 Which statement does *not* apply to feedback?
 A Communication through speech
 B Communication through letters and internal reports
 C Communication through meetings
 D Communication through advertisements in newspapers and magazines

19 Which management / motivational theorist did *not* recognise the need for communication as a source of motivation in the workplace?

   A A. Maslow

   B F. Taylor

   C E. Mayo

   D C. Handy

20 Which of the following is *not* a consequence of poor communication in the workplace?

   A Low morale

   B Reworking

   C Lower productivity

   D Lower absenteeism

Unit 2.4 Leadership and Management

Task 1: Complete the missing words

Management is the process of getting things done through other people in order to achieve the a...... and o................. of a business. This is likely to involve planning, organizing, coordinating, commanding and controlling the various operations and resources within an organization. .... (MBO) is a term coined by Peter Drucker that involves managers setting objectives for themselves, based on the overall objectives of the organization.

Managers and leaders adopt different styles to tackling organizational objectives and strategies. For example, ... leaders make decisions independently of others and delegate very little responsibility to their subordinates. By contrast, ... leaders encourage others to be involved in the decision making process by a process of consultation and considering the views of the workforce before implementing any changes. Managers may adopt a .... approach when inducting new staff or when dealing with staff with personal difficulties.

Douglas McGregor claimed that .... managers are authoritarians who assume that employees need constant supervision because they lack ambition and prefer to be told what to do. These managers also believe that workers are lazy and dislike work and are essentially motivated only by money. By contrast, a .... manager believes workers do have initiative, do want to take responsibility for their own work and can be creative if motivated (perhaps by praise and recognition for their achievements).

There are various factors that influence a person's style of management and leadership. These influences include: the nature of the .... (e.g. whether it is routine or a major undertaking that requires strategic leadership), the nature of the .... (e.g. experience, qualifications, training and personality) and the organizational .... (i.e. the "way" things are done in the organization).

Task 2: Explanations

a Outline three core competencies that leaders must develop to be successful.

_____

_____

_____

_____

b What do you think management guru Warren Bennis meant when he said, "Failing organizations are usually over-managed and under-led".

_____

_____

_____

_____

c Outline two factors that could influence someone to adopt an autocratic leadership style.

_____

_____

_____

_____

d   If a leader needs to seek the advice from others when making a key strategic decision, is this a sign of weak leadership?

_____

_____

_____

_____

Task 3: True or false?

		True / False
a	The best managers are those who are compassionate towards their staff.	
b	Leaders are the people at the top of an organization.	
c	Theory Y managers are likely to adopt a democratic style of management.	
d	Theory X managers tends to involve and trust their employees.	
e	According to F.W. Taylor, workers respect autocratic bosses.	
f	Since laissez-faire managers allow employees to work towards their own objectives, this tends to be the most effective management style today.	
g	Corporate culture is an important factor in determining a person's management and leadership style.	
h	A paternalistic management style tends to be suitable when dealing with new and inexperienced workers.	

Task 4: Crossword – Leadership and management

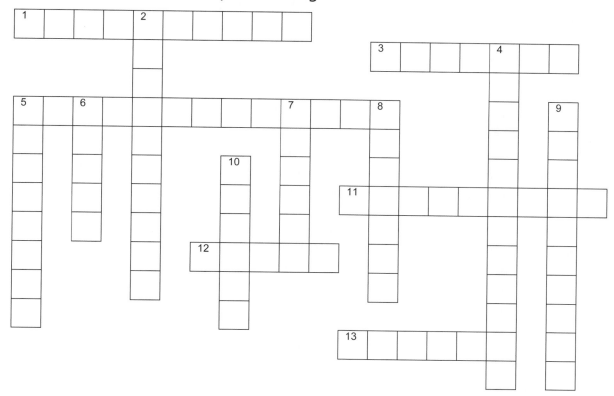

Clues Across

1 An authoritarian style of management
3 Contingency theorist who suggested that there is no single best way to lead
5 Managers that act in what they believe to be in the best interest of their subordinates
11 Senior managers make these types of decisions
12 Targets and objectives, in short, should be: specific, measurable, agreed, realistic and time constrained
13 The lowest level of management, also known as supervisory management

Clues Down

2 One of the core functions of management as suggested by Henri Fayol
4 Style of management most suited to firms with highly skilled and competent staff
5 All managers participate in this key function
6 Theories that suggest a person's leadership/management style depends on their characteristics
7 The highest ranking level of managers
8 The customs and norms within an organization
9 Management style will affect the level of this driving force in an organization
10 An official leader or manager established by the organization, rather than through natural flair or charisma

Task 5: Multiple choice

1 The management style that sees the leader allowing subordinates to achieve targets in their own way is known as

   A Laissez-faire
   B Democratic
   C Autocratic
   D Paternalistic

2 Which management or leadership style is most suitable during a hostile takeover?

   A Authoritarian
   B Autocratic
   C Democratic
   D Paternalistic

3 Types of leaders include all the following except

    A Born

    B Natural

    C Formal

    D Autonomous

4 Which statement does *not* apply to an autocratic style of management?

    A Senior management make all the key decisions

    B Management closely supervise and direct workers

    C Suitable when quick decision making is required

    D Useful when working with highly skilled workers

5 Autocratic leaders excel when dealing with

    A Experienced workers who want to have an input

    B An unexpected crisis

    C A very small number of workers

    D Trusted employees

6 A democratic management style exists when managers

    A Trust their employees

    B Direct workers

    C Ignore the views of subordinates

    D Leave workers to achieve their targets in their own way

7 Which of the following is *not* a feature of the Classical Management school of thought, as advocated by F.W. Taylor and H. Fayol?

    A Division of labour

    B Tall organizational structures

    C Delegation and Empowerment

    D Authoritarian management style

8 The leadership style that encourages workers to make decisions which management will listen to is called

    A Theory X

    B Theory Y

    C Democratic

    D Paternalistic

9 …………. believed that managers can have one of two distinct views of the …………. and motivation of employees at work.

    A Herzberg, movement

    B McGregor, attitudes

    C Maslow, attitudes

    D Taylor, movement

10 Which of the following factors does *not* affect the style of management or leadership?

   A The nature of the task

   B Personality

   C Corporate culture

   D Specialization and division of labour

11 When critical decisions need to be made, which style of management and leadership is most appropriate?

   A Laissez-faire

   B Democratic

   C Autocratic

   D Paternalistic

12 Which statement does *not* apply to a Theory X view of workers?

   A Workers do not like work

   B Staff must be closely monitored as they are lazy

   C Employees try to avoid responsibility

   D Workers can be fulfilled by their work

13 An autocratic leader does *not*

   A Make all the decisions alone

   B Delegate much, if any, responsibility to subordinates

   C Maintain overall authority in decision making

   D Work well during a time of emergency or crisis

14 Which type of leader consults their staff and makes decisions based on such consultation?

   A Paternalistic

   B Situational

   C Contingent

   D Democratic

15 Which of the following statements relates best to an authoritarian manager or leader?

   A Centralized decision-making

   B Considers the welfare of the workforce before making key decisions

   C Will consult staff before making key decisions

   D Makes decisions that are believed to be in the best interest of the staff, even if this means being unpopular

16 **[HL Only]**   A key difference between managers and leaders is that

   A Managers have subordinates

   B Managers simply conform to the organizational culture

   C Leaders are those at the very top of an organization

   D Managers are professionally qualified

17 **[HL Only]**   Leadership is *not* directly concerned with

   A Training and developing people

   B Guiding people

   C Influencing people

   D Cohesiveness in the workplace

18 [HL Only]   According to management guru Peter Drucker, which of the following is *not* a key function of management?

   A Setting clear goals

   B Organizing people

   C Measuring performance

   D Controlling people

19 [HL Only]   Theories that suggest managers are 'born' rather than 'made' are known as

   A Contingency theory

   B Situational theory

   C Trait theory

   D Innate theory

20 [HL Only]   What is the phrase used to refer to the notion that there is no single 'best' management or leadership style, but that it depends on a range of interconnected factors?

   A Eventuality theory

   B Contingency theory

   C Circumstantial theory

   D Trait theory

Unit 2.5 Motivation

Task 1: Complete the missing words

Motivation refers to the w..................... to work. This drive can come from the satisfaction of work itself (such as teaching or photography) and/or from the desire to achieve one's goals and .... (such as to earn money, to gain recognition or to accomplish greatness).

The two broad methods of motivation are .... methods (e.g. salaries, commission, bonuses and profit sharing) and .... methods (e.g. praise, recognition and job enrichment).

Poor motivation can be costly to a business since a...................., labour ...., wastage and disciplinary problems are likely to increase. By contrast, the q.................... and q.................... of output are likely to fall.

Abraham Maslow's theory of motivation differs markedly from that of F.W. Taylor's in that .... considered the human side of work. He put forward the theory of a hierarchy of human needs which have to be fulfilled in order to motivate a person. At the base of the hierarchy are .... needs and at the top of the hierarchy are .... needs.

Herzberg argued that .... must be met to prevent dissatisfaction, but they alone do not motivate workers. Having a well paid job but without a sense of recognition or opportunities for advancement, Herzberg argued, will not motivate an individual.

Task 2: The theorists' theories

a   Place the following examples of Herzberg's motivators and hygiene factors under the correct headings:

- Achievement
- Administration and company policies
- Advancement
- Job security
- Opportunity for promotion
- Paperwork

- Recognition
- Responsibility
- Rules and regulations
- Self-realization
- Supervision
- Wages

Hygiene Factors	**Motivators**

b Arrange the following factors into Maslow's hierarchy of needs.

- Acceptance
- Accomplishment
- Achievement
- Affection
- Basic necessities
- Biological needs
- Develop fully

- Fitting in
- Friendship
- Fulfil potential
- Group identity
- Job security
- Pay
- Personal growth

- Predictability
- Reputation
- Respect
- Responsibilities
- Stability
- Status
- Steady job
- Survival

Self-actualization	Esteem Needs	Love and Belonging Needs	Safety Needs	Physiological Needs

c Place the following examples of management attitudes of workers under the correct heading of McGregor's Theory X and Theory Y.

- Ambitious
- Avoid responsibility
- Enterprising
- Enthusiastic

- Laziness
- Need to be managed
- Passive
- Seek responsibility

Theory X	Theory Y

d Name the motivational theorist from the given clues.

Theorist	Content of Theory
	Two-factor theory based on hygiene factors and motivators
	Hierarchy of needs ranging from physiological needs to self-actualization
	Standardized output for piece rate payment based on scientific management techniques
	Theory X and Theory Y attitude of management
	Human relations in the work place

Task 3: True or false?

		True / False
a	Herzberg argued that motivators are more important than hygiene factors to motivate a workforce.	
b	Contrary to what Maslow predicted, not all people want promotion or want to stretch themselves to self-actualization.	
c	Overtime pay usually attracts a higher rate of pay.	
d	According to Herzberg, hygiene factors such as pay can cause motivation.	
e	Taylor's scientific management considered the human aspects of the workplace.	
f	McGregor's Theory X suggests that people are motivated by financial rewards.	
g	Job enrichment means allowing employees more control over their jobs.	
h	Performance-related pay links payment to the level of profits of the firm.	
i	In McGregor's theory, there is no such thing as 'Theory X workers'.	
j	**[HL Only]** Mayo argued that teamworking can be obstructive as well as constructive.	

Task 4: Vocabulary quiz

Identify the key terms from the clues given. *Hint*: the answers are in alphabetical order.

Key Term	Definition
	Payment system often used for sales people that rewards employees according to number of products that they sell.
	Income received after tax deductions are made from an employee's salary or wages.
	Perks received by employees in addition to their standard wage or salary, e.g. free meals and work uniforms.
	Form of motivation (and multi-skilling) that involves increasing the number of tasks involved in a particular job.
	Method of motivation that gives employees more responsibilities and decision-making power.
	Form of motivation that involves employees working on different tasks in turn, in order to add some variety to their job.
	Payment system based on rewarding employees who meet certain targets; used by managers to gauge the level of individual employee performance.
	Payment system that pays employees according to how much they actually produce or sell, thereby giving workers an incentive to be more productive.

Task 5: Distinguish between ...

a   Gross pay and Net pay

_____

_____

b   Overtime and Bonuses

_____

_____

c   Job Enrichment and Job Enlargement

_____

_____

d   Motivation and Movement, according to Professor Frederick Herzberg

_____

_____

e   Time-based and Piece-rate payment systems

_____

_____

Task 6: Explain ...

a   Which of the following ought to be high (from an organization's viewpoint)

   i   Absenteeism

   ii Labour turnover

   iii Staff retention

_____

_____

b   How grievances and poor punctuality are both indicators of poor motivation in a business

_____

_____

c   Two non-financial incentives used by retailers to motivate their workers

_____

_____

d   How and when each of the following leadership and management styles can motivate a workforce

   i   Autocratic

_____

_____

   ii Democratic

_____

_____

iii Paternalistic

_____

_____

e   Why improved maternity and paternity rights should help to reduce the absence rate of workers with young children

_____

_____

f   Why *job enrichment* is more motivating than job enlargement or job rotation

_____

_____

g   How contributions to a worker's pension (retirement) fund is an example a hygiene factor

_____

_____

h   Why share options schemes may not necessarily motivate a firm's workforce

_____

_____

i   How a lack of motivation can cause diseconomies of scale. What assumption is being made?

_____

_____

_____

_____

j   Two advantages to a business that encourages teamwork

_____

_____

_____

_____

k   Two drawbacks of using Performance Related Pay as a payment system

_____

_____

l   Two forms of non-financial motivators

_____

_____

Task 7: Odd one out (Herzberg)

Explain the odd one out in each case.

a	Responsibility	Sense of achievement	Nature of the job	Work conditions
b	Wages	Supervision	Responsibility	Company policies
c	Responsibility	Company policies	Autonomy	Authority

Task 8: Multiple choice – Motivation theory

1 Reasons why people work do *not* include
- **A** To earn money to satisfy physiological needs
- **B** To feel a sense of belonging
- **C** To improve a firm's presenteeism
- **D** To maintain skills and employability

2 A highly motivated workforce will *not* lead to higher levels of
- **A** Productivity
- **B** Quality
- **C** Labour turnover
- **D** Customer service

3 Which scenario below is *not* an example of absenteeism?
- **A** With consent given by his employer, Patrick attends his son's graduation ceremony overseas
- **B** Martin wakes up late and decides it would be better to stay at home as the boss does not like poor punctuality
- **C** Camilla delegates her work to an assistant as she attends all-day meetings with her branch manager
- **D** Pearl does not feel well and has permission from the doctor to refrain from attending work

4 A demotivated workforce is likely to lead to lower levels of
- **A** Absenteeism
- **B** Staff turnover
- **C** Recruitment costs
- **D** Presenteeism

5 The theorist who suggested that workers are paid for the work that they do rather than for their mental ability was
- **A** F.W. Taylor
- **B** A. Maslow
- **C** D. McGregor
- **D** E. Mayo

6 Which of the following characteristics cannot be applied to Taylor's scientific management?
- **A** Workers are motivated by pay
- **B** Piece rate can motivate
- **C** Workers specialize in order to maximize output
- **D** Workers are motivated by the working environment

7 Which statement cannot be applied to Maslow's theory of levels of needs?
- **A** People are not simply motivated by money alone
- **B** Coined the term self actualisation as the ultimate goal for workers
- **C** People can move down as well as up the hierarchy of needs
- **D** Lower level needs do not have to be satisfied in order to be motivated

8   According to Maslow, identification with and acceptance from a particular group can help to meet which level of human needs?

   A   Friendship

   B   Social

   C   Teamworking

   D   Security

9   Which option is least likely to be a potential problem for Chan & Wong Solicitors if they use financial incentives to improve motivation at the firm?

   A   It may be seen as divisive rather than promoting teamwork

   B   It may reduce the quality of service since solicitors now focus on output

   C   It may prove to be very expensive for the partners

   D   It may encourage employees to be less productive

10   Which of the following features is *not* part of Taylorite theory?

   A   High degree of specialization and division of labour

   B   Job satisfaction

   C   Alienation of the workforce

   D   Repetitive jobs

11   Making a job more challenging is an example of

   A   Job enrichment

   B   Job enlargement

   C   Job retrenchment

   D   Job rotation

12   Empowerment could be seen if a manager

   A   Provides more interesting jobs for subordinates

   B   Delegates decision making to subordinates

   C   Allows teams to work on a task

   D   Gives workers more jobs to complete

13   According to Frederick Taylor, the best type of payment system would be one based on

   A   The qualifications and experience of a worker

   B   Piece-rate payment systems

   C   Time-based payment systems

   D   Wages and salaries

14   Which of the following is a 'maintenance' factor under Herzberg's theory of motivation?

   A   Advancement

   B   Personal Growth

   C   Salary

   D   Responsibility

15   According to Professor F. Herzberg, which of the following is *not* a 'hygiene' factor?

   A   Status

   B   Recognition

   C   Job security

   D   Policies and administration

16 Costs of high absenteeism in the short-run include all the following except

    A The cost of hiring temporary cover staff

    B Loss of business due to lower productivity

    C The costs of reduced morale and teamworking

    D The costs of recruitment and training

17 Which statement below is *not* necessarily a benefit of having a highly motivated workforce?

    A Increased rivalry among the workforce

    B Higher productivity

    C Lower levels of absenteeism

    D Reduced levels of staff turnover

18 Which statement applies to F.W. Taylor's theory of motivation?

    A Workers should specialize so that they can master their craft

    B Workers should be empowered to increase their motivation

    C Non-financial motivators are as important as financial ones

    D Financial rewards are not enough to motivate the workforce

19 According to Frederick Herzberg, any factor that does *not* directly motivate a worker, but when *not* present will directly de-motivate someone, is known as a

    A Demotivator

    B Motivator

    C Hygiene factor

    D Two-factor theory

20 According to Herzberg, factors that can actually motivate an employee to work harder include

    A Pay

    B Working conditions

    C Recognition

    D Job security

21 Which theorist did *not* emphasize communication as an important motivator in the workplace?

    A Herzberg

    B Taylor

    C Maslow

    D Mayo

22 Which of the following is *not* part of F.W. Taylor's scientific management theory?

    A Piece rate

    B Performance related pay

    C Specialization

    D Teamworking

23 According to McGregor's Theory X and Theory Y, which of the worker attitudes listed below do managers hold if they are Theory Y?

    A Are lazy and therefore need to be controlled

    B Are keen to excel

    C Need threats and punishments

    D Are motivated by financial rewards

24 Several groups of people are unlikely to go through Maslow's hierarchy of needs in a chronological order. Which group is the exception to this?

   A Charity volunteers

   B Priests and other religious leaders

   C Freelance writers

   D Television celebrities

25 Which statement best applies to Taylor's theory of motivation?

   A Managers should closely monitor, control and supervise their employees

   B Management approach that sees workers as being lazy and motivated by monetary reasons

   C Workers are motivated by job enrichment, teamworking and job enhancement

   D Workers are motivated by the same types of needs and wants

26 Security needs in Maslow's hierarchy of needs can be met by offering employees

   A Piece rate payments

   B Money

   C Employment contracts

   D Promotion

27 Which facility would *not* directly address a worker's social needs as a form of motivation?

   A Staff Christmas party

   B Departmental offices and work areas

   C Observation of anti-racial discrimination laws

   D Training and development opportunities

28 **[HL Only]**   According to McClelland, people who are more concerned with gaining success rather than social relationships have which need?

   A Need for power

   B Need for affiliation

   C Need for achievement

   D Need for triumph

29 **[HL Only]**   Which of the following is *not* a feature of Mayo's Human Relations School of thought?

   A Group dynamics

   B Teamworking

   C Employees have non-financial needs, rather than just financial ones

   D Working conditions do have a significant impact on motivation levels

30 **[HL Only]**   Which of the following is *not* a feature of Elton Mayo's theory of motivation?

   A Money is a key motivator

   B Group norms and work culture

   C Human relations at work

   D Managers taking an interest in their staff

31 **[HL Only]**   Theories that seek to explain the factors that actually motivate workers are called

    A Appraisal meeting

    B Content theories

    C Motivation theory

    D Process theories

32 **[HL Only]**   Which theorist suggested that employees are most motivated and productive when they are able to have opportunities for social interaction with their peers and when managers take an interest in their wellbeing?

    A Elton Mayo

    B David McClelland

    C Chris Argyris

    D Meredith Belbin

33 **[HL Only]**   The Hawthorne experiments of Mayo did *not* conclude that motivation is linked to

    A Whether management take an interest in their workers

    B Whether the social needs of workers are considered

    C The working conditions, such as the level of lighting

    D Group dynamics and leadership styles

34 **[HL Only]**   J.S. Adams's equity theory states that

    A Fairness exists when employers recognise efforts with rewards

    B Inequality will drive workers to perform better to secure pay rises

    C Every worker should be paid the same salary and benefits

    D Employees who treat their employers well will be rewarded

Task 9: Multiple choice – Motivation in practice

1 Which statement below cannot be applied to wages?

    A Are a type of time-based payment system

    B Are normally paid per hour worked

    C Overtime at a rate higher than the wage rate has to be paid for any extra hours worked

    D Does not motivate workers to be extra productive

2 The payment system that rewards workers for each item that they produce or sell is known as

    A Commission

    B Piece rate

    C Time rate

    D Royalty payments

3 If an employee works beyond their contracted hours (as shown on their contract of employment) then they are usually entitled to

    A Time in lieu

    B Overtime pay

    C Holiday pay

    D Promotion

4   A consequence of paying workers by piece rate is that
   A It directly rewards people for their time spent working
   B Workers may ignore quality due to the emphasis on speed of work
   C It promotes team building
   D High quality work is recognised and rewarded accordingly

5   McDonald's pay their crew member staff different hourly wage rates. Which factor is *not* a legal justification for doing so?
   A Levels of responsibility
   B Extent of experience
   C Different geographical location
   D Different gender

6   Which payment system is preferred for situations where quality and output cannot be easily measured?
   A Piece rate
   B Performance related
   C Time based
   D Output based

7   Satine is in a job where she is paid $15 per hour. This week, she has worked for 38 hours and has done an additional 5 hours overtime at 'time and a half'. Calculate her gross pay for the week.
   A $570.00
   B $607.50
   C $645.00
   D $682.50

8   Using the information in Question 7, calculate Satine's annual salary excluding overtime pay.
   A $109,915
   B $103,740
   C $29,640
   D $18,532

9   The payment system whereby employees receive a share of the company's profits is known as
   A Performance related pay
   B Profit-related pay
   C Dividends
   D Retained profits

10 Which of the following is *not* a valid reason for pay differentials?
   A Conditions of supply and demand vary in different industries
   B Gender differences in diverse jobs
   C Different levels of cost of living in different regions
   D Rewarding people with higher levels of qualifications

11 The method of motivating workers by giving them more responsibilities and more interesting tasks is known as

   A Job enlargement

   B Job rotation

   C Job enrichment

   D Delegation

12 Job enlargement is *not* concerned with

   A Boosting the morale of workers

   B Increasing the number of tasks performed by an employee

   C Giving workers more complex tasks to do

   D Multi-skilling the worker

13 The name given to the overall package of pay and perks of a job is

   A Payment systems

   B Contract of employment

   C Remuneration

   D Earnings

14 Teamworking does *not* allow a business to benefit from

   A Lower labour turnover

   B Lower absenteeism

   C Higher labour productivity

   D Shorter decision-making time

15 The method of motivation that encourages workers to decide on their work priorities and to come up with their own solutions to problems is known as

   A Laissez-faire management

   B Delegation

   C Empowerment

   D Performance appraisal

16 Which of the following is an advantage of piece rate?

   A Motivates highly skilled workers

   B Suitable for people who have autonomy in decision making

   C Acts as an incentive to work

   D Encourages teamworking

17 The non-financial motivation method that involves broadening the number of tasks that are completed by a worker is called

   A Job enrichment

   B Job enlargement

   C Job rotation

   D Job description

18 Disadvantages of piece rate do *not* include

A Difficulty in differentiating between the productivity of workers

B Negative impact on quality as staff take shortcuts to complete tasks

C Can be divisive and discourage teamworking

D Difficult to apply to many professions where measuring output is complicated

19 Which of the following is a financial method of motivation?

A Job enrichment

B Delegation

C Empowerment

D Medical allowances

20 Which of the following would *not* be classed as a fringe benefit?

A Company car

B Salaries

C Private education allowance

D Work uniform (clothing)

Unit 2.6   Organization and Corporate Culture

Task 1: Complete the missing words

Corporate culture refers to the shared b..............., v............. and a................ of the people within an organization. These norms subsequently determine the way in which the business operates on a daily basis. It also underpins corporate strategy and the corporate image. Senior management will seek to create a positive culture in order to .... workers to deliver a first-rate product or service to their customers. If people are united and committed to the organization's .... statement, then a strong corporate culture will be developed.

Task 2: True or false?

		True / False
a	Corporate culture informs employees of how things are done in the organization.	
b	A culture gap tends to help strengthen corporate culture.	
c	An understanding and awareness of organizational culture is important to managing change.	
d	Senior management strive to determine corporate culture to reflect the aims and objectives of the organization.	
e	Within an organization only one culture is likely to exist.	
f	Culture frequently resembles the existing management style in an organization.	
g	Charles Handy suggested that there is no direct link between a firm's organizational structure and its corporate culture.	
h	If there is a lack of trust within the organization, then this provides a valid reason for a necessary change in the corporate culture.	
i	The leaders of an organization establish organizational culture through their actions and direction.	

Task 3: Multiple choice

1   Corporate culture is based on

   A   The management and leadership styles in an organization

   B   The set of beliefs and values held by the people within an organization

   C   The traditions and customs of a country

   D   The rules and regulations set out by the prevailing government

2   Cultural intelligence refers to a person's

   A   Cultural awareness

   B   Ability to fit into a culture

   C   Willingness to comply with a particular culture

   D   Lack of enthusiasm to blend into a culture

3   When management and employees of an organization have different beliefs and values, there is said to be

   A   Conflict

   B   An industrial dispute

   C   A culture gap

   D   Corporate diversity

4 Which of the following is the least likely reason for a necessary change in corporate culture?

   A The existing culture restricts organizational growth

   B Conflict is not being managed within the organization

   C There is a high degree of staff absenteeism and staff turnover

   D Profits are in decline

5 Although ……………… have a large part in defining and determining organizational culture, all ……………… contribute to the culture.

   A Directors, Stakeholders

   B Shareholders, Stakeholders

   C Executives, Employees

   D Leaders, Stockholders

6 Organizational cultural change is often met with resistance for several reasons. Which option is *not* one of the valid reasons?

   A Employees fear change

   B A significant event, such as a financial crisis, has occurred

   C Stakeholders have not been informed or consulted

   D People find it difficult to change their behaviour to suit the newly desired culture

7 Which of the statements below does *not* apply to team norms?

   A Team members interact with one another based on an established culture

   B Effective interpersonal communication among members is critical to the functioning of the team

   C The way in which a team makes decisions influences the degree of the team's success

   D Team norms do not change over time

8 An organization without an agreed framework for decision making is likely to face the potential of

   A Misunderstandings and conflict

   B Industrial action

   C Redundancies and retrenchment

   D Prompt decision making

9 An organization with one dominant decision-making individual or group has what type of culture?

   A Task culture

   B Power culture

   C Person culture

   D Role culture

10 According to John Kotter and James Heskett (1992), which type of culture is resistant to change since people hold negative views about organization culture change?

   A Inert cultures

   B Adaptive cultures

   C Command and rule cultures

   D Process cultures

Unit 2.7 Employer and Employee Relations

Task 1: Explain one reason why ...

a Corporate culture affects the degree of employer and employee relations at work

_____

_____

b Workers might join a trade union

_____

_____

c There has been a decline in union membership in many parts of the world

_____

_____

d Conflict might exist in the workplace

_____

_____

e Avoidance is a source of conflict resolution

_____

_____

f Reducing or eliminating conflict in the workplace is in the best interest of an organization

_____

_____

Task 2: Explain the difference between ...

a Conciliation and Arbitration

_____

_____

b Consultation and Negotiations

_____

_____

c Industrial action and Strike action

_____

_____

d Work to rule and Go slows

_____

_____

Task 3: Multiple choice

1   Which of the following is *not* considered to be a form of industrial action?

   A   Strike action

   B   Work to rule

   C   Renegotiations

   D   Go slow

2   Employers' associations

   A   Represent the views and interests of businesses within a specific industry

   B   Represent the views of the media regarding an employer's treatment of its workers

   C   Deal with public relations issues in order to gain positive media coverage

   D   Employ highly skilled managers to intimidate or pressure employees to cease any form of industrial action

3   Conflict is unlikely to be caused by which of the below factors?

   A   Disagreements between different stakeholders

   B   Incompatibilities between stakeholder groups

   C   Internal politics in the workplace

   D   Compromise between different stakeholder groups

4   Unmanaged conflict can become a problem for businesses. Which of the following is unlikely to result from conflict in the workplace?

   A   Higher absenteeism

   B   Lower staff morale

   C   Industrial action

   D   Higher capacity utilization

5   The power of a labour union is *not* necessarily strengthened by which factor?

   A   The number of members

   B   Government legislation

   C   The quality of the leadership of the union

   D   Public support

6   Employees who follow all the policies and procedures with the objective of slowing down production are engaged in which form of industrial action?

   A   Work to rule

   B   Overtime ban

   C   Voluntary strike action

   D   Go slow

7   The negotiations and relationship between trade union members and their employer is known as

   A   Collective bargaining

   B   Industrial relations

   C   Arbitration

   D   Conciliation

8   Conciliation does *not* consider

    A Negotiations

    B Win-win situations

    C Litigation

    D Cooperation

9   Arbitration is the process of

    A Settling disputes by using an agreed arbitrator whose decision is legally binding

    B Using an external arbitrator to negotiate a win-win outcome for those in conflict

    C Improving working conditions in the workplace to benefit both employers and employees

    D Resolving conflict by hiring a mediator to advice on the outcome of a dispute

10 Trade unions do *not* have a direct role in

    A Negotiations

    B Collective bargaining

    C Mediation

    D Counselling

Unit 2.8   Crisis Management and Contingency Planning

Task 1: True or false?

		True / False
a	Contingency planning is also known as crisis management.	
b	Careful planning can help an organization to reduce the risks of a crisis.	
c	Having insurance is a possible solution to a crisis situation.	
d	It is important to select an appropriate team to handle disaster recovery.	
e	Crisis management is about dealing with threats and disasters facing a business.	
f	Public relations play a vital part in crisis management.	
g	Irrespective of their size, all businesses face threats.	
h	A properly prepared contingency plan is the first step to being prepared to manage a crisis.	

Task 2: Case study

Mattel Inc., the world's leading toy manufacturer, faced more than 28 product recalls during 2007, upsetting consumers and retailers alike. It was reported that a public relations team of 16 people was set up to call reporters, alongside news releases and teleconference calls. The Mattel CEO, Robert Eckert, also conducted television interviews and telephone calls with individual reporters. By summer 2008, the product recall crisis seemed to have been forgotten.

a   What is meant by a product recall and why is it an example of a crisis?

_____

_____

_____

_____

b   Identify three stakeholder groups from the case study.

_____

_____

c   Outline two reasons why crisis management and contingency planning are important to global multinationals such as Mattel Inc.

_____

_____

_____

_____

_____

_____

Task 3: Multiple choice

1   The way in which an organization responds to a crisis is known as

    A   Contingency planning

    B   Crisis management

    C   Operational management

    D   Emergency backup plan

2   Which of the following is least likely to cause a crisis in an organization?

    A   Sexual harassment

    B   Bribery

    C   Hostile takeover

    D   Rumours and gossiping

3   A public relations disaster can be prevented by

    A   Having a larger marketing budget

    B   Preparing a better business plan

    C   Crisis prevention through foresight

    D   Crisis prevention through hindsight

4   Which event is least likely to be part of a large publishing firm's contingency plan?

    A   Copyright infringement

    B   Information sabotage

    C   Product recall

    D   Absenteeism issues

5   Which of the following is *not* a potential drawback of contingency planning?

    A   The incident planned for might not ever happen

    B   The incident planned for is less likely to occur over time

    C   Contingency planning is expensive

    D   Some risks are not quantifiable, thereby making planning difficult

6   Quantifiable risks are those that are

    A   Expensive to insure against

    B   Financially measurable threats

    C   Difficult or impossible to measure

    D   Natural in occurrence

7   Which of the following is most likely to be an unquantifiable risk for a cinema?

    A   Loss of valuable stock

    B   Assault from customers

    C   Natural disaster that destroys the cinema

    D   Copyright infringements

8   The systematic attempt to prevent or to manage crises should they occur is known as

   A   Workforce planning

   B   Damage recovery management

   C   Contingency planning

   D   Crisis management

9   Which of the following is *not* a characteristic of a crisis to an organization?

   A   Unpredictable

   B   Unexpected

   C   Threatening

   D   Element of surprise

10   A crisis is least likely to occur in which one of the following cases?

   A   Disgruntled customers

   B   Industrial espionage

   C   Public relations savvy managers

   D   Conflict

ACCOUNTS AND FINANCE

UNIT

3

Unit 3.1   Sources of Finance

Task 1: Classification of income and expenditure

Classify the following into either assets or liabilities and whether they represent an expense or a source of income (revenue) for a large book publisher by marking the appropriate columns.

Category	Asset	Liability	Expense	Revenue
Bank interest receivable				
Bank loans				
Bank overdrafts				
Debentures				
Insurance premiums				
Motor vehicles				
Rent accruals				

Task 2: Vocabulary quiz

Identify the key terms from the clues given. *Hint*: the answers are in *reverse* alphabetical order.

Key Term	Definition
	The most common type of shares issued by a limited company, which gives holders voting rights and dividends based on the company's profits.
	A long-term source of finance which requires the borrower to provide property and land as collateral (security guarantee) to the lender in case the borrower defaults on the loan.
	Refers to the generation of finance from within an organization's own resources and funds, e.g. retained profits, working capital or the sale of fixed assets.
	Refers to the original sales of a company's shares on to the stock market, by offering its shares to the general public for the first time.
	This source of finance allows firms the chance to use assets without having to pay for them in one lump sum. Once the final repayment (instalment) has been made, the asset legally belongs to the business.
	A long-term source of finance which gives holders a fixed rate of return (interest) but without any ownership or voting rights.
	The spending on items considered as fixed assets, such as: land, buildings, machinery and motor vehicles.

Task 3: Consider the differences between …

a   Capital and revenue expenditure

_____

_____

b   Short-term and long-term finance

_____

_____

c   An overdraft and bank loan

_____

_____

d   A loan and a mortgage

_____

_____

e   Ordinary share capital (equity) and Preference share capital

_____

_____

f   Ordinary shares and Debentures

_____

_____

g   Debt finance and equity finance

_____

_____

h   Owners' capital and loan capital

_____

_____

Task 4: True or false?

		True / False
a	Directors own the money of incorporated firms and use these on behalf of their shareholders.	
b	Government grants and subsidies are a form of external financing.	
c	Personal finance is the cheapest source of finance.	
d	Share issues by a company are considered to be internal sources of finance.	
e	Collateral acts as security to the lender in case debtors default on their loans.	
f	Capital expenditure is used to pay for the working capital of an organization.	
g	High loan capital means the business is likely to suffer during times of rising interest rates.	

h	Overdrafts are easier to obtain than most other forms of external finance.	
i	Permanent capital is equal to the value of shareholders' funds, i.e. share capital and reserves.	
j	It is best if a business reduces obtaining finance from a variety of sources simply because this raises its financial risks.	
k	Venture capitalists tend to invest their money in medium to large-sized businesses since they have the best investment track record.	

Task 5: Multiple choice

1   Which of the following is the most feasible reason for using personal finance?

   A Insufficient internal sources of finance

   B Insufficient external sources of finance

   C There is no interest obligation

   D To please the owners / shareholders of a company

2   Advantages of growth through share issue include all those listed below except

   A Less risk due to the spreading of risks amongst shareholders

   B An extra source of funds

   C Control of the company is diluted

   D Form of motivation for employees who own shares in the company

3   Which of the following is a drawback to a business that issues debentures?

   A There is dilution of control

   B There is a dilution of ownership

   C Lenders do not have any voting rights

   D The value of liabilities increases

4   An advantage of using internal funds to purchase a new office building could include

   A Limited impact on the firm's working capital

   B Lower level of gearing

   C Dilution of ownership

   D Increased value of fixed assets

5   Businesses might choose to use external sources of finance because

   A There are no interest charges

   B Potential cash flow problems are avoided

   C There is insufficient retained profit

   D There is an expected increase in interest rates

6   Which of the following is *not* a source of external financing for a public limited company?

   A Overdraft

   B Debentures

   C Retained profits

   D Share capital

7 Debenture holders

  A Own a part of the company in which they hold debentures

  B Are paid a return from the profits of the company

  C Receive payments from companies before any shareholders

  D Are represented as current liabilities on the company's balance sheet

8 Which of the following is the least likely source of funds for a non-profit organization?

  A Fund-raising events

  B Charitable donations

  C Brand recognition

  D Sponsorship deals

9 Advantages of internal finance do *not* include

  A Greater flexibility in use of finance

  B Greater choice of finance

  C No need to go through administrative procedures

  D Tax concessions for the use of internal profits

10 Which of the following is *not* a source of finance for an ordinary partnership?

  A Secured bank loans

  B Sale and Leaseback

  C Debt factoring

  D Initial public offer

11 Which statement below best describes hire purchase?

  A The hiring of equipment for a period of time

  B Repaying loans by making fixed regular payments

  C Hiring out equipment as a source of finance

  D Differs from leasing in that ownership occurs with the last instalment

12 Which of the following does *not* describe a clear difference between debenture holders and share holders of a company?

  A Voting rights in the company

  B Ownership of the company

  C Interest and dividends as a form of financial return

  D Impact on the company's working capital

13 The contract used to raise finance by selling the freehold to an asset and then renting it back immediately on a long-term basis is known as

  A Sale and leaseback

  B Working Capital

  C Fixed assets

  D Trade creditors

14 The debt factoring service that allows the client to be protected against bad debts is known as

  A Overdraft

  B Non-recourse factoring

  C Discount factor

  D Collateral

15 Mei Ling Photography Corp. has a cash flow deficit of $85,000. If it has debtors to the value of $100,000, what is the maximum charge that a factoring service could impose to make this source of finance feasible?

   A 5%

   B 10%

   C 15%

   D 20%

16 Which statement does *not* apply to the use of sale and leaseback?

   A The firm can continue to use the asset it has sold and leased back

   B The value of fixed assets remains unchanged since the firm keeps use of the asset

   C The firm can carry on trading as if nothing has happened

   D The finance released through the sale improves the firm's liquidity position

17 Which source of finance below would best be described as loan capital?

   A Preference shares

   B Equity

   C Debentures

   D Debt factoring

18 There must be sufficient finance to pay for the daily running of the business. This money is known as

   A Working capital

   B Work-in-progress

   C Reserves

   D Buffer stocks

19 Debentures can best be described as a form of

   A Short-term loan with variable interest rates

   B Medium-term loan with variable interest rates

   C Long-term loan with a fixed interest rate

   D Long-term security giving the holder part ownership of the business

20 Which of the following is a disadvantage of leasing capital equipment?

   A It is cheaper in the long run to buy capital equipment

   B Capital equipment needs replacing if technology is changing rapidly

   C The management of cash flow is easier with regular repayments

   D The firm might not have sufficient funds to purchase the equipment

Unit 3.2   Investment Appraisal

Task 1: Complete the missing words

Investment is the .... used to increase the productive capacity and operations of a business. It can include the purchase of buildings, equipment, machinery and motor vehicles.

The .... method of investment appraisal measures the length of time it takes for an investment project to generate enough profit to recoup the cost of investment. It is quick to calculate but does not tend to favour .... projects, i.e. those with a long payback period.

[HL Only]   The average rate of return (ARR) measures how much profit, on average, an investment project generates as a .... of the investment cost.

Net present value looks at the .... cost of money because money received in the future is worth less than it is today. Discounted cash flow is another technique which is based on the opportunity cost of money and .... forecasts.

Task 2: Explain the relationship between ...

a   [HL Only]   The discount rate and the Net Present Value

_____

_____

b   Contribution and Payback period

_____

_____

c   Interest rates and the level of gearing

_____

_____

Task 3: True or false?

		True / False
a	Considering the future value of money, the higher the interest rate, the less money is worth if received in the future.	
b	Investment appraisal is a forward-looking decision-making tool.	
c	Discounting is important to account for the future value of cash flows.	
d	Payback uses the flow of profits to assess the feasibility of an investment.	
e	The Accounting rate of return and the Net present value methods of investment appraisal are expressed in percentage terms.	
f	[HL Only] The higher the value of the ARR, the more financially feasible an investment project tends to be.	
g	The NPV is relatively easier to calculate than the Payback period.	

Task 4: Vocabulary quiz

Identify the key terms from the clues given. *Hint*: the answers are in alphabetical order.

Key Term	Definition
	An investment appraisal technique that calculates the typical annual profit of an investment project. It is expressed as a percentage of the initial sum of money invested.
[HL Only]	An investment appraisal technique that reduces the value of the money that a business receives in future years. This is done as there is an opportunity cost to money (which loses its value over time) and in order to give a current (present-day) value for the expected future returns.
[HL Only]	An investment appraisal technique that calculates the total discounted cash flows, minus the initial cost of an investment project. If this figure is positive, then the project is viable and should be undertaken (on financial grounds).
	Cost measured in terms of the next best alternative that is foregone when a choice is being made, e.g. money today can be either spent for immediate benefit or saved for the future.
	An investment appraisal technique which estimates the length of time that it will take to recoup the initial cash outflow of an investment project.
	Judging whether an investment project is worthwhile through non-numerical means, such as whether an investment decision is in line with the corporate culture.

Task 5: Multiple choice

1   Which of the following investment appraisal techniques uses time as its unit of measurement?

   A Payback period

   B Average Rate of Return

   C Net Present Value

   D Internal Rate of Return

2   Which of the following is an example of investment in a business context?

   A Paying out dividends to shareholders

   B Placing money into a savings bank account

   C Purchasing new machinery

   D Borrowing money from a bank

3   **[HL Only]**   If interest rates are 5% per annum, what is the present value of $100 received next year?

   A $105.00

   B $95.00

   C $96.45

   D $95.24

4 **[HL Only]**   Which term below refers to the numerical value used to work out the present value of a sum of money received in the future?

   A Net cash flow

   B Discounted cash flows

   C Discount factor

   D Net present value

5 **[HL Only]**   Which of the following is *not* a quantitative investment appraisal technique?

   A ARR

   B PED

   C IRR

   D DCF

6 The accounting rate of return is also known as

   A Average rate of return

   B Annual rate of return

   C Effective rate of return

   D Discounted rate of return

7 Which quantitative factor applies to a firm considering investing in a new computerised stock control system?

   A Staff training issues

   B Upgradability and compatibility with future technologies

   C The firm's cash flow position

   D Time to implement new system

8 Which of the following is *least* important for firms that use the payback period method of investment appraisal?

   A Firms that focus on time as a priority

   B Firms that see liquidity as more important than profitability

   C Firms seeking an early return on their investment

   D Firms that focus on profitability rather than short-term cash flows

9 Which statement below does *not* apply to the payback period?

   A Time, rather than profit, is the centre of attention

   B The timing of the net cash flows are largely ignored

   C It is simpler to calculate and understand than other investment appraisal methods

   D Favours projects that have high profit quality

10 Which business situation would *most* suit the payback period of investment appraisal?

   A A new multi-complex cinema and entertainment centre

   B The building of a new international airport

   C Manufacturing processes where technology changes frequently

   D Firms that can afford to use cash to raise the necessary finance for investment

11 Payback is least favourable as a measure of investment appraisal when

    A The costs of investment need to be regained quickly

    B Firms have a poor cash flow position

    C Projects are expected to return a profit in the medium to long term

    D Time is of major priority

12 The net present value of an investment helps to establish the value of ………. flows of income and expenditure. The ……….. the discount factor, the lower the value of future cash flows in real terms.

    A Future, lower

    B Future, higher

    C Present, lower

    D Present, higher

13 Qualitative factors to consider in an investment appraisal do *not* include

    A The aims and objectives of the business

    B The culture of the organizations, such as level of employee participation

    C Alternative investment projects and their potential yields

    D External factors such as the state of technology

14 Which limitation applies specifically to the Average Rate of Return?

    A It ignores the timing and pattern of cash flow

    B It does not consider quantitative factors

    C It focuses on time rather than profit

    D It favours only short-term investment projects

15 Factors that affect a multinational corporation's investment decision are least likely to include

    A Its business objectives

    B Effects on human relations

    C Leadership and management styles

    D Unquantifiable risks

16 **[HL Only]** Which investment appraisal method is *not* a measure of profit or profitability?

    A Average rate of return

    B Payback period

    C Discounted cash flows

    D Net present values

17 **[HL Only]** Limitations of the Net Present Value method of investment appraisal do *not* include

    A The difficulty of forecasting cash flows in the distant future

    B NPV can be tedious to calculate

    C Changes in interest rates will alter the NPV figure

    D It accounts for medium-term to long-term projects

18 The ARR can best be described as an investment appraisal technique that

    A Calculates the average annual profit of a project as a percentage of the initial investment cost

    B Calculates the annual profit of a project as a percentage of the initial investment cost

    C Measures the accounting period for which a project will break-even and earn a profit

    D Measures the future value of net cash flows for an investment project

19 Which of the following is *not* a qualitative factor affecting investment appraisal?

    A New competing products being launched by rival firms

    B The state of the economy, such as the rate of inflation and unemployment

    C Forecast changes in interest rates that affect the real value of money

    D Uncertainties about the future

20 [HL Only]   Which statement does *not* apply to the use of net present values?

    A NPV relies on the use of discounted cash flows

    B The NPV value will fall if interest rates rise

    C NPV is expressed in percentage terms to allow for easier benchmarking

    D A positive NPV means that the investment decision is justifiable on financial grounds

Unit 3.3   Working Capital

Task 1: Vocabulary quiz

Identify the key terms from the clues given. *Hint*: the answers are in alphabetical order.

Key Term	Definition
	Quantitative technique used to predict how cash is likely to flow into and out of a business in the foreseeable future.
	These are short-term assets of an organisation that can be converted into cash within a year, e.g. stocks, debtors and cash.
	Money owed to creditors and financiers that is repayable within the next twelve months.
	This dilemma is caused by a lack of cash because the firm's net cash flow is negative.
	This is calculated by using the formula cash inflow minus cash outflow per time period, i.e. the difference between receipts and payments.
	The yield that is calculated by subtracting total costs from total revenues.
	Refers to the cash inflow into a business.
	Refers to the spending on goods and services that have been consumed (or will be shortly) rather than on the purchase of fixed assets.
	Also known as 'net current assets', this is the daily amount of money that is available for business operations.

Task 2: Outline ...

a   Two reasons why a new restaurant is likely to have poor net cash flow in the first months of setting up business

_____

_____

b   Three different ways that a business might be able to improve its cash flow position

_____

_____

_____

c   The difference between sales and profits

_____

_____

d   Why debtors are considered to be an asset

_____

_____

e   Two ways that a hotel might be able to improve its cash flow

_____

_____

f   Two major causes of cash flow crises for a business

_____

_____

Task 3: Explain the difference between …

a   A cash flow statement and a cash flow forecast

_____

_____

b   Debtors and creditors

_____

_____

_____

c   Current assets and fixed assets

_____

_____

d   Cash and profits

_____

_____

Task 4: True or false?

		True / False
a	Without stocks, a business would not be able to survive for very long.	
b	The higher the liquidity of an asset, the easier and quicker it is to turn it into cash.	
c	A highly geared firm has a large percentage of interest-bearing capital.	
d	There is a positive correlation between cash flow and profit.	
e	Negotiating shorter payment periods with creditors helps to improve cash flow.	
f	Working capital can be negative, but only in the short term.	
g	Net current assets is another name for working capital.	
h	A cash flow forecast is used to show the final profit in a trading period.	
i	Profit is more important than cash to a business.	
j	Tight credit control is vital if a business wants to avoid cash flow problems.	
k	A cash flow statement records the flows of cash in and out of a business over the past year.	
l	Working capital is the cash that a firm has for its day-to-day running.	

Task 5: Crossword – Cash flow

Clues Across

1   The most liquid of all assets (4)

2   The situation when cash inflow equals cash outflow (7)

5   Another term for revenue or turnover (5)

6   Another term for closing balance - …. Cash flow (10)

8   Firms or people who owe money to another firm (7)

9   Part of a firm's liquid assets (6)

12 Where a business attempts to expand too rapidly, without a sufficient financial base (11)

13 One of the largest outflows for most businesses (5)

15 Firms that are highly …… have to pay out a lot in interest payments (6)

17 What a firm faces in extreme and prolonged cases of cash flow problems (10)

18 A possible interest-bearing solution to resolving a cash flow deficit, offered by banks (5)

20 To predict the cash flows of a business (8)

22 Cash leaving a firm (7)

23 Another term for spare or surplus cash that could be better used elsewhere (6)

Clues Down

1   Difference between the cash flowing into and out of the business (4,4)

3   Value of the closing balance when opening balance + receipts = payments (3)

4   Factoring services will insist on charging this (3)

6   Cash balance at the end of the month (7)

7   These could be sold to raise cash (6)

10 Service that allows a business to withdraw more money than exists in its account (9)

11 Sale and ……… – a method of increasing cash inflow (9)

14 Banks do this to firms to help them with a cash flow problem (4)

16 Do not confuse this with cash (6)

19 Another name for revenue ..… (5)

21 Business rates are an example of this type of cash outflow (3)

Task 6: Multiple choice

1 Working capital is defined as

    A The difference between the assets and liabilities of a business

    B The money available to a business for its day-to-day operations

    C The money that belongs to a business

    D The difference between a firm's total assets and its immediate debts

2 Which statement below does *not* apply to the components of capital in an incorporated company?

    A Long-term bank loans

    B Cash used to buy current assets

    C Share capital

    D Retained profits

3 Which of the following is *not* a sign of a business that is overtrading?

    A A fall in the value of trade debtors due

    B Higher than usual levels of work-in-progress

    C Higher than usual levels of finished goods

    D An increase in liquidity problems

4 Which of the following is a current liability?

    A Stocks

    B Overdrafts

    C Cash

    D Debentures

5 Debtors are

    A People or businesses that have sold items on credit

    B Individuals or businesses in debt

    C Customers who have bought items but did not pay for them in cash

    D Parties who have sold items and are awaiting cash payment

6 Currents assets do *not* include

    A Unfinished goods

    B Unsold finished goods

    C Raw materials

    D Copyright and Patents

7 The legal responsibility of a business for the money it owes to other parties in more than 12 months is called

    A Long-term loans

    B Long-term liabilities

    C Security or Collateral

    D External sources of finance

8 Which of the following is *not* a current liability?

    A Interest charges

    B Creditors

    C Work-in-progress

    D Corporation tax

9   What would a 'contingency fund' be used for?

   A To help expansion plans

   B To improve working capital during unforeseen events

   C To pay suppliers and other creditors

   D To entice customers to pay by cash rather than on credit

10 The financial document that shows how cash has flowed into a business and what it has spent the cash on is known as

   A Cash flow forecast

   B Cash flow statement

   C Cash and expenditure account

   D Profit and loss account

11 Which of the following would *not* be classed as a current asset?

   A Debtors

   B Stocks

   C Creditors

   D Cash at the bank

12 Identify the fixed asset from the options below.

   A Work-in-progress

   B Fixtures and fittings

   C Raw materials

   D Cash in hand

13 The majority of stock held by a retailer will be in the form of

   A Working capital

   B Cash

   C Work-in-progress

   D Finished goods

14 Working capital is calculated by

   A Net assets less Net liabilities

   B Total cash inflow less total cash outflows

   C Current assets less Current liabilities

   D Opening balance plus Net cash flow

15 In the worst case scenario, firms struggling to survive may sell what in order to generate working capital?

   A Some net assets

   B Certain fixed assets

   C Various current liabilities

   D Debentures

16 One major purpose of constructing a cash flow forecast is to

   A Show the value of profit made by a firm at the end of each trading session

   B Identify the sources of cash inflows and cash outflows

   C Provide a planning and decision-making tool for managing a firm's cash flows

   D Present information on the sources of sales revenues and costs of production

17 Which of the following is likely to improve a firm's cash flow position?

    A Greater value of debtors

    B Longer credit periods

    C Paying for items by use of hire-purchase

    D Higher interest rates

18 Causes of cash flow crises are *not* likely to include

    A Tight credit control

    B Overtrading

    C Money tied up in stocks and inventory

    D High gearing

19 Hanley Sports Equipment has produced a cash flow forecast which predicts a closing year end balance of $50,000. The firm later discovers that an order for $8,000 was ignored from the sales figure and that a utility bill for $3,000 was unpaid. What should the new closing balance be?

    A $61,000

    B $55,000

    C $39,000

    D $3,000

20 What is the annual cash flow for Reed & Co, given the following financial information?

    Reed & Co. Annual Cash Flow Statement (excerpts):

        Opening balance:$35,000

        Receipts: $95,000

        Payments: $50,000

    A $45,000

    B $75,000

    C $80,000

    D $110,000

Unit 3.4 Budgeting [Higher Level Extension]

Task 1: Complete the missing words

.... refers to the art of financial control in an organization. A .... is a financial plan which an organization strives to achieve and allows the organization to check its progress against the budgeted figures. A budget should reflect the .... of an organization, e.g. if the firm plans to replace expensive capital equipment, then this amount should be incorporated into the budget plan. Budgets can be used for any quantitative variable, e.g. s........., c........., profit, staffing, advertising expenditure and capital expenditure.

In reality, it is likely that there will be deviations from the budget plan. Variance analysis is a management tool used to calculate differences in the actual and budgeted figures. A .... variance occurs when the .... outcome is better than the budgeted (planned) outcome. An .... variance occurs when the actual outcome is .... than the budgeted plan. Variance analysis also looks at the reasons for the differences that occur and can therefore be a useful analytical tool in assessing the success of a strategy.

Task 2: Calculations and analysis

a Complete the missing figures for Danny and Demi's Hair Salon Ltd. The first one has been completed for you.

Variable	Budgeted ($)	Actual Outcome ($)	Variance ($)	Variance (F/A)
Wages	4,000	4,200	200	Adverse
Salaries	4,500	4,500		
Stock	1,800	1,850		
Revenue	15,750		290	Favourable
Direct costs		2,950	250	Favourable

b Give two examples of 'stock' that are likely to be held by Danny and Demi's Hair Salon Ltd.

_____

_____

c Give two examples of direct costs likely to be incurred by Danny and Demi's Hair Salon Ltd.

_____

_____

Task 3: Explain ...

a The difference between adverse budgets and budget deficits

_____

_____

b The difference between budgets and forecasts

_____

_____

    c   Why 'positive' variances do not exist in budgeting

    d   One key advantage of zero budgeting

Task 4: Multiple choice

1   Which of the statements best describes a budget?

    A The money available to a business on a day-to-day basis

    B The financial plan for the next 12 months

    C Forecast inflows and outflows of cash over the next 12 months

    D The spending allowance of the different departments of a business

2   Budgets do *not* cover the issue of

    A Output levels

    B Sales

    C Workforce planning

    D Operational expenses

3   The budgeting system that requires budget holders to justify the money that they wish to spend is known as

    A Tight budgeting

    B Loose budgeting

    C Zero budgeting

    D Budgetary constraint

4   The budget cycle usually lasts for what period of time?

    A 1 day

    B 1 month

    C 6 months

    D 12 months

5   The difference between actual results and budgeted results is known as

    A Variance

    B Discrepancy

    C Conflict

    D Deviation

6   Which of the following is *not* a direct function of budgeting?

    A To ensure that managers plan ahead

    B To assess performance-related pay of managers

    C To anticipate costs and revenues

    D To review progress on a regular basis

7 Which type of budget allows an organization to adjust to changes in the business environment?

   A Zero budgeting

   B Flexible budgets

   C Master budgets

   D Contingency budgets

8 When actual advertising costs are more than the budgeted figure, there is said to be a(n)

   A Favourable variance

   B Positive variance

   C Negative variance

   D Unfavourable variance

9 Which of the following is *least* likely to be a factor that affects how a budget is set?

   A Historical benchmarking

   B Negotiations

   C Budget holder's length of experience

   D Availability of finance

10 When cash receipts are higher than expected or staffing costs are less than anticipated, the result is

   A Higher profitability

   B Higher revenue expenditure

   C Favourable variances

   D Shorter cash-flow cycle

Unit 3.5   Final Accounts

Task 1: Complete the missing words

All businesses need to be accountable to their owners. One way to do this is to produce final accounts on an annual basis. The .... shows a snapshot of a firm's assets and liabilities at a particular point in time (usually the end of the trading year). .... are the property of a business, i.e. the resources that it owns. .... refer to the money owed by a firm to other people or organizations.

The profit and loss account is a record of the firm's trading activities over a period of time (usually .... months). It is split into .... parts. The trading account shows the value of a firm's gross profits, i.e. the difference between .... and cost of sales. .... are the overheads of a business that account for the difference between a firm's .... profit and its operating profit. The remaining part of the account shows the amount of .... that is distributed to shareholders.

[Higher Level Extension]

When reporting fixed assets, some businesses will include .... assets. They are non-physical assets that have a monetary value, such as g................., t................. and investments in other companies.

Depreciation refers to the .... in the value of .... assets over time. Depreciation is most commonly calculated by spreading the .... cost of a fixed asset over its expected useful lifespan, taking into account the scrap (or ....) value of the asset. This method of calculating depreciation is known as the .... method. For example, if a printing machine costing $10,000 with an expected residual value of $1,000 is depreciated over its forecast 5-year lifespan, then the annual depreciation amounts to .... Some fixed assets, such as land and buildings, can increase in value over time (known as ....), although they still incur maintenance and repair costs.

Task 2: True or false?

		True / False
a	Sole traders and partnerships are not required by law to publish their final accounts publicly.	
b	Bank overdrafts and creditors are examples of current liabilities.	
c	Cash flow forecasts are historical statements showing the movement of cash in a business over time.	
d	All fixed assets depreciate over a long period of time.	
e	Appreciation refers to an increase in the value of an asset over time.	
f	Net assets refers to the difference between a firm's total assets and its current liabilities.	
g	Capital expenditure can be interpreted via a Balance Sheet.	
h	Historic cost is the original price that a firm paid for the purchase of a fixed asset.	
i	The profit figure shown in a profit and loss account is an accurate estimate which may be revised at a later date.	
j	It is not a legal requirement for all companies to show their shareholders the sources and uses of finance.	
k	[HL Only] Motor vehicles tend to depreciate most in value at the beginning of their useful life.	
l	[HL Only] The reducing balance method of depreciation reduces the value of an asset by a fixed amount of the book value of the asset.	
m	[HL Only] LIFO stock valuation will tend to reduce the tax bill for businesses.	

Task 3: Explain one ...

a   Advantage of distributing a larger percentage of net profits as retained profit rather than allocating a greater amount to shareholders

_____

_____

b   Difference between operating profit and profit before tax

_____

_____

c   Difficulty when comparing financial data between different businesses

_____

_____

d   Reason for incorporated companies having to prepare and publish their final financial accounts

_____

_____

e   Reason why a balance sheet must balance

_____

_____

f   Difference between fixed and current assets

_____

_____

g   [HL Only]   Reason why assets might depreciate in value over time

_____

_____

h   [HL Only]   Way in which depreciation affects the profit and loss account

_____

_____

i   [HL Only]   Reason why motor vehicles are usually depreciated using the reducing balance method rather than the straight line method

_____

_____

Task 4: Formulae

Identify the key terms from the clues given. *Hint*: the answers are in *reverse* alphabetical order.

Formula	Key Term
Opening stock *plus* purchases *less* closing stock	
Net profit after tax *less* Retained Profit	
Sales revenue *less* cost of goods sold	
Gross profit *less* expenses	
Net profit *less* Gross profit	
Sales revenues *less* total costs of production	
Net profit after tax and interest *less* Dividends	

Task 5: Calculations

a   Slater Tiling Company has an opening stock of $35,000, a closing stock of $30,000, and has purchased stock during the year costing $95,000. Calculate the firm's cost of goods sold (COGS).

_____

_____

b   Ortega Clothing Company has expenses of $123,000 and a net profit of $321,000. Calculate the firm's gross profit.

_____

_____

c   Hooper Toys Ltd purchases goods at $10,000 and manages to sell these for $18,000. State the:
i   cost of goods sold
ii   the sales revenue
iii   the gross profit

_____

_____

d   Complete the missing figures from the accounts of Constance Curtains Ltd.

Profit And Loss Account		Balance Sheet	
	$		$
Turnover	800,000	Fixed assets	350,000
Cost of goods sold	450,000	Current assets	250,000
Gross profit	i	Current liabilities	180,000
Expenses	85,000	Assets employed	iv
Operating profit	ii	Loan Capital	150,000
Corporation tax	53,000	Share Capital	v
Net profit	iii	Capital employed	vi

e   Work out the value of net profit from the following information:

Turnover $200,000
Cost of sales $80,000
Expenses $45,000
Non-operating income $24,000
Interest receivable $1,200
Interest payable $13,000

_____

_____

_____

_____

f   **[HL Only]**   Assume that Pitarch Car Hire Co. bought a vehicle for $35,000 with an expected life of 4 years. Its residual value is estimated to be $7,000. Calculate the straight line depreciation per year.

_____

_____

g   **[HL Only]**   Assume that equipment bought by a manufacturer costing $15,000 has a useful life of 5 years. Annual depreciation is charged at 40%. Calculate the book value of the asset after two years.

_____

_____

Task 6: Multiple choice – Profit and loss

1   The Trading Account gives details of
  A The current value of the organization
  B Overheads and other costs of production
  C The cost of goods sold
  D The net profit (or loss) made during a trading period

2   If expenses are greater than gross profit for a business, then the business
  A Has performed well
  B Has made an overall loss
  C Can distribute a share of the profit to shareholders
  D Has a positive net profit balance

3   In which account would overheads and expenses appear?
  A Appropriation account
  B Balance sheet
  C Profit and Loss account
  D Trading account

4   Which statement below *cannot* be applied to Gross Profit?
  A Expressed as a percentage to allow for historical and inter-firm comparisons
  B Appears on the Trading Account
  C Calculated as Sales less Cost of Goods Sold
  D Calculated by Sales less Cost of Sales

5 Which of the following items does *not* appear in a profit and loss account?

 A Expenses

 B Overheads

 C Machinery and equipment

 D Cost of goods sold

6 The profit and loss account

 A Lists all assets of a business during a trading period

 B Lists all revenue and expenditure of a business over a trading period

 C Calculates the gross profit of a business

 D Shows the amount of money owed to other businesses

7 Calculate the cost of sales from the following information: Cost of stock per unit = $20, Units of stock purchases = 800, Closing Stock = 300 units and Opening stock = 250 units.

 A $5,000

 B $15,000

 C $22,000

 D $27,000

Questions 8–10 refer to the information below.

Cost of sales	$35,000
Expenses	$25,000
Non-operating income	$10,000
Retained profit	$20,000
Tax	$15,000
Turnover	$100,000

8 What is the firm's gross profit?

 A $30,000

 B $35,000

 C $65,000

 D $70,000

9 What is the firm's net profit?

 A $50,000

 B $40,000

 C $30,000

 D $20,000

10 What is the firm's total dividend payout to shareholders?

 A $5,000

 B $10,000

 C $15,000

 D $20,000

11 Which of the following is a business *not* legally obliged to report?

A   Balance Sheet

B   Cash flow forecast

C   Profit and loss account

D   Cash flow statement

12 On a profit and loss account, dividends represent

A   The share of 'after-tax profits' that is distributed to shareholders

B   The share of net profits that is reinvested by the business

C   The difference between tax and interest payments

D   The difference between retained profit and expenses

13 The appropriation account does *not* show

A   Corporation tax

B   Dividends

C   Interest charges

D   Retained profits

14 A business earns $200,000 in sales, has expenses of $80,000 and cost of goods sold are $90,000. What is its gross profit?

A $30,000

B $110,000

C $170,000

D $120,000

15 A firm could increase its gross profit by

A   Cutting advertising expenditure

B   Using cheaper suppliers

C   Reducing management salaries

D   All of the above

16 Which of the following would be shown as an exceptional item on a profit and loss account?

A   The sale of property above its book value

B   The closure of a factory

C   Costs of restructuring management

D   Marketing and administration costs

17 Which of the following would *not* be classed as an expense in the profit and loss account?

A   Marketing costs

B   Direct costs

C   Indirect costs

D   Rent and administration

18 Net profit and operating profit are equal when there is an absence of which option below?

A   Expenses

B   Dividends to shareholders

C   Non-operating income and interest

D   Corporation tax

19 Where is revenue earned from holding shares in other companies that have paid out dividends recorded?

   A Trading Account

   B Appropriation Account

   C Investments

   D Non-operating income

20 Use the following information to work out the profit on ordinary activities before tax:

      Cost of sales $50,000

      Expenses $30,000

      Interest payable $1,000

      Non-operating income $5,000

      Turnover $100,000

   A $14,000

   B $15,000

   C $20,000

   D $24,000

21 Expenses are the

   A Indirect costs of trading activities

   B Direct costs of trading activities

   C Indirect costs of non-trading activities

   D All non-trading costs

22 Expenses do *not* include

   A Rent

   B Insurance premiums

   C Depreciation

   D Cost of sales

23 Non-operating income does *not* include

   A Interest payments from bank deposits

   B Dividend payments from shareholdings in other companies

   C Rental income from property owned overseas

   D Revenue from discounted products sold during an end-of-season sale

24 Gross profit less expenses plus non-operating income gives

   A Net profit

   B Gross profit

   C Operating profit

   D Retained profit

25 Interest payable means

   A Interest paid to lenders, such as banks

   B Interest received from bank deposits

   C Interest payments to debenture holders

   D Interest charged to debtors for late payment

Task 7: Multiple choice – Balance sheet

1   Which of the following statements does *not* usually apply to fixed assets?

    A   Assets owned by a business for more than 12 months

    B   Assets that a business intends to keep for more than 12 months

    C   Assets that generate cash sales for a firm

    D   Brands, logos and slogans

2   Current assets do *not* include

    A   Inventories

    B   Work in progress

    C   Debtors

    D   Creditors

3   Publication of final accounts include all the following statements except

    A   Profit and loss account

    B   Balance sheet

    C   Cash flow forecast

    D   Cash flow statement

4   Suppliers would be interested in the final accounts of a business in order to

    A   Assess business profitability and performance

    B   Calculate corporation tax liabilities

    C   Negotiate pay and productivity agreements

    D   Secure external sources of finance

5   Physical assets tend to depreciate over time. Which asset below does *not* generally follow this trend?

    A   Cash

    B   Land

    C   Machinery

    D   Brands

6   Net assets is calculated by

    A   Fixed assets + Current assets

    B   Fixed assets – Current assets

    C   Fixed assets + Working capital

    D   Fixed assets – Working capital

7   Which of the following is *not* considered to be a fixed asset?

    A   Land

    B   Machinery

    C   Debtors

    D   Trademarks

8   Fixed assets include all the following except

    A   Physical assets

    B   Intangible assets

    C   Investments

    D   Finished stocks

9 Money owed to other people or organizations are shown in a balance sheet as
   A Current liabilities
   B Net assets
   C Debts
   D Liabilities

10 Which statement about tangible assets is true?
   A They are physical assets owned by the firm for long-term use
   B Assets that depreciate in value over time
   C They represent the use of funds of a business
   D Assets that are not always possible to value such as brand names

11 Which of the following equations is found in a balance sheet of a public limited company?
   A Net Assets = Long-term Liabilities + Owners' Equity
   B Total Assets = Total Liabilities
   C Net assets = Current Liabilities + Working capital
   D Net current assets = Liabilities + Shareholders' Funds

12 Which of the following is most likely to be a long-term business liability?
   A Overdraft
   B Loans
   C Debentures
   D Hire purchase

13 Current assets do *not* include
   A Working capital
   B Tax reimbursements
   C Cash at bank
   D Semi-finished goods

14 Capital employed does *not* include the calculation of
   A Reserves
   B Shareholders Equity
   C Fixed assets
   D Preference shares

15 Work out the value of net current assets from the information given:
   Land = $50,000
   Creditors = $10,000
   Share capital = $200,000
   Cash = $10,000
   Stock = $20,000
   Overdrafts = $25,000
   Loans = $30,000
   A ($5,000)
   B $30,000
   C $200,000
   D $215,000

16 If a firm buys a delivery vehicle with cash, how will this be reflected in the balance sheet?

   A An increase in the value of net assets employed

   B An increase in the value of fixed assets with a corresponding fall in the value of cash

   C An increase in the net cash outflow

   D An increase in depreciation charges and a fall in the cash balance

17 Which item appears on the balance sheet of a sole trader?

   A Shareholders funds

   B Capital and reserves

   C Capital employed

   D Debentures

18 In which final accounts would you find 'Shareholders' Funds'?

   A Balance Sheet

   B Profit and Loss account

   C Trading account

   D Cash Flow Statement

19 Which of the following items is *not* found in a balance sheet?

   A Liabilities falling due after one year

   B Trade creditors

   C Intangible fixed assets

   D Net profits before interest and tax

20 The main purpose of constructing a balance sheet is to

   A Provide financial data and information for shareholders

   B Show the value of a business at a particular point in time

   C Allow stakeholders and investors to assess a firm's liquidity

   D Identify the correct amount of tax liability based on the market value of the business

21 **[HL Only]** A patent

   A Provides legal protection for an inventor to prevent others from copying it

   B Provides legal protection against those copying the printed work of others

   C Gives the exclusive right to the use of a brand name, symbol or slogan

   D Is a type of physical fixed asset that does not necessarily appear on a balance sheet

22 **[HL Only]** An increase in the value of certain fixed assets, such as land and buildings, is known as

   A Depreciation

   B Appreciation

   C Advances

   D Enlargement

23 **[HL Only]** Which of the following is *not* an intangible asset?

   A Investments

   B Goodwill

   C Cash deposits at the bank

   D Patents, copyrights and trademarks

24 [HL Only]   Intangible assets include all the following except
 A Brand names
 B Goodwill
 C Services
 D Copyrights

Questions 25 and 26 refer to the following information.

De Melo Consultancy uses the declining balance method to depreciate its fixed assets. The firm purchases computers worth $300,000 and uses a depreciation rate of 30%. The computers are expected to last 5 years before being replaced.

25 [HL Only]   What is the net book value of the computers after two years?
 A $90,000
 B $120,000
 C $147,000
 D $180,000

26 [HL Only]   What would the annual depreciation charge be if De Melo Consultancy had used the straight line depreciation method for the computers?
 A $60,000
 B $90,000
 C $120,000
 D $300,000

27 [HL Only]   Which statement *cannot* be applied to goodwill?
 A It is a type of intangible asset
 B It includes the value of labour such as their market value if they were headhunted
 C It is the value of the firm's customer and staff loyalty
 D It can only be truly measured once a business is sold at a premium to its book value

28 [HL Only]   Intangible assets are
 A Non-physical fixed assets that add value to a business
 B Physical fixed assets that add value to a business
 C Services that add value to a business
 D Current assets that add value to a business

29 [HL Only]   Suppose a firm has opening stock of $5,000, purchases of $6,000 and cost of goods sold valued at $8,000. What is the value of its closing stock?
 A $3,000
 B $7,000
 C $9,000
 D $19,000

30 [HL Only]   The main benefit to a firm using the LIFO, rather than the FIFO, method of stock control is that
 A LIFO is easier to calculate than FIFO
 B LIFO gives priority to older stock to be to issued for production
 C FIFO is not suitable for most large businesses
 D FIFO produces less tax efficient valuation of stocks

Unit 3.6   Ratio Analysis

Task 1: Complete the missing words

Ratio analysis is useful for anyone who has a direct interest in the financial performance of a business. These people or organizations are known as the stakeholders of the business, such as:

- .... – These people or organizations will be interested in the return on their investment, so will be interested in financial ratios related to the firm's profitability.

- .... – The personnel will also be interested in the profitability of the organization since this will influence pay and job security.

- .... – The leadership team will be interested in financial ratios in order to gauge performance and to aid decision making.

- .... and .... – These stakeholders will be interested in the liquidity of the business which affects its ability to pay for their goods.

- .... – Banks, for instance, will be interested in the longer term liquidity position of a business to judge its ability to repay loans.

- .... – Rival firms will be interested to gauge the performance of the business. This is often used as part of its benchmarking practice.

- .... – The state will want to look at the financial performance of a business to ensure that proper accounting procedures are being followed (to prevent fraudulent reporting of finances) and to calculate the correct amount of tax due by the firm.

Task 2: Explain ...

a   How high gearing might be profitable for some businesses

_____

_____

b   The error(s) made by students in each of the following statements about the definition of 'return on capital employed'

   i   "Profit expressed as a return on capital employed"

_____

_____

   ii   "Profit made is greater than capital spent"

_____

_____

   iii   "Profit that covers all your set-up costs"

_____

_____

   iv   "Shows the amount of profit that a firm makes"

_____

_____

c   Why highly geared firms are more exposed to the pressures of an economic downturn

_____

_____

d **[HL Only]**   Given the limited information below, which company has performed better in the short term and which company has the better potential in the long term?

	Alpha Toys Ltd	Beta Toys Ltd
Dividend per share	$0.50	$0.50
Earnings per share	$0.60	$0.80
Current price per share	$12.00	$13.00

_____

_____

_____

_____

e   Given the limited information below, which company represents the higher risk to a potential investor?

	Jake Clothing Ltd	Luke Clothing Ltd
Capital employed	$1,000,000	$1,200,000
Debentures	$100,000	$150,000
Mortgage	$350,000	$280,000

_____

_____

_____

_____

_____

_____

_____

_____

Task 3: Vocabulary quiz

Identify the key terms from the clues given. _Hint_: the answers are in _inverse_ alphabetical order.

Key Term	Definition
	Ratios that look at the level and value of a firm's profits.
	Measures overall profit (after all costs have been deducted) as a percentage of sales revenue.
	Ratios that look at a firm's ability to pay its debts.
	Ratios that look at how well a firm is using its resources.
[HL Only]	The ratio that measures the number of days it takes, on average, for a business to pay its lenders.

Task 4: True or false?

		True / False
a	A highly geared firm is generally more vulnerable to changes in interest rates.	
b	A highly geared firm is more at risk during a recession.	
c	Shareholders are more concerned about dividend earnings than capital growth.	
d	It is considered too risky to invest in a firm with a gearing ratio of 50% or above.	
e	Capital employed is the sum of equity capital plus long-term liabilities.	
f	Profits tend to be more volatile in businesses with high gearing.	
g	Highly geared firms are seen as being a risky investment as they are unlikely to make much profit.	

Task 5: Fill in the blanks

a   When the value of a firm's stock (inventory) increases, the acid test ratio will ………

b   A firm that has a long working capital cycle will tend to prefer to use the ……… ……… ratio in order to measure its liquidity.

c   When stock levels fall, the stock turnover ratio will ……….

d   **[HL Only]**   When the value of creditors rise, the creditor days ratio will ……….

Task 6: Odd one out

Select the odd one out from each of the options below.

a	Acid test	Gearing	Net profit margin	Current
b	Debtor days	Stock turnover	Gross profit margin	ROCE
c	ROCE	EPS	GPM	NPM
d	Cash	Stocks	Debtors	Creditors

Task 7: High or low?

Explain whether the following financial ratios should, ideally, be high or low.

a   **[HL Only]**   Creditor days

_____

_____

b   **[HL Only]**   Debtor days

_____

_____

c   Stock turnover

_____

_____

d   [HL Only]   EPS

_____

_____

e   ROCE

_____

_____

f   Gearing (*Hint*: 'it depends')

_____

_____

Task 8: Complete the table

Use the information given in the table below to identify the ratio and the type of ratio (profitability, liquidity, efficiency or shareholder ratio). *Hint*: the ratios are listed in *reverse* alphabetical order.

Formula	Ratio	Type of Ratio
Cost of sales / Stock		
(Net profit / Capital Employed) * 100		
(Net profit / Sales revenue) * 100		
(Gross profit / Sales revenue) *100		
Profit before tax / number of shares issued		
(Dividend per share / Market share price) * 100		
(Debtors / Sales revenue) * 365		
Current assets / Current liabilities		
(Creditors / Cost of Sales) * 365		
Current assets less Stock / Current liabilities		

Task 9: Multiple choice

1   All of the following are financial performance ratios except
   A Return on capital employed
   B Stock turnover
   C Labour turnover
   D Acid test ratio

2   Calculating the return on capital employed provides information on a firm's
   A Profitability
   B Return to potential shareholders
   C Liquidity or solvency
   D Effective use of capital resources

3   Which of the following is not a short-term liquidity ratio?
   A Acid Test
   B Current
   C Gearing
   D Quick

4 Which ratio would a business prefer not to be very high in value?

    A Return on capital employed

    B Gross profit margin

    C Acid test

    D Stock turnover

5 The acid test ratio can be used to identify a firm's

    A Profitability

    B Ability to pay its short-term debts

    C Ability to pay its long-term debts

    D Return on the use of fixed assets

6 The net profit margin can be used to identify a firm's

    A Profitability

    B Degree of overhead control

    C Ability to pay its debts

    D Amount of return to its shareholders

7 If a business has gross profit of $3 million and sales revenue of $5 million and expenses of $1 million, then the net profit margin would be

    A 40%

    B 60%

    C $1 million

    D $2 million

8 The ratio that measures profit in relation to the size of a business is known as

    A Net profit margin

    B Net profit before interest and tax

    C Gross profit margin

    D Return on capital employed

9 If a business had gross profit of $100m, overheads of $10m and capital employed of $200m, then the return on capital employed would be

    A 45%

    B 50%

    C 55%

    D 220%

10 Which of the following ratios can be 'too high' (undesirable) from a firm's point of view

    A Return on capital employed

    B Current ratio

    C Net profit margin

    D Creditor days

11 Capital employed is equal to

    A Shareholders' funds plus Long-term liabilities

    B Shareholders' funds less Long-term liabilities

    C Net Assets less Liabilities

    D Assets employed less Long-term liabilities

12 Which statement below cannot be applied to short-term liquidity ratios?

   A Involves calculating the ability of a business to pay its short-term debts

   B Looks at the ratio of current assets to current liabilities

   C Looks at the level of gearing in a firm

   D Measures the ability of a firm to meet its short-term liabilities

13 The ability of a firm to pay its short-term debts without having to sell any of its stock is shown by which ratio?

   A Quick ratio

   B Current ratio

   C Liquidity ratio

   D Shareholders ratio

14 Stock turnover is the ratio used to measure

   A The number of times a business sells its stocks in a year

   B How much stock is purchased each year

   C The stock levels in relation to the sales turnover made

   D Sales revenue as a percentage of the average stock level

15 Which business would be least pleased with a stock turnover ratio of 95 days?

   A Honda cars

   B Boeing aircraft

   C McDonald's restaurants

   D Reebok sports apparel

16 **[HL Only]**   If a firm has dividends per share of $0.50 and the current market price is $4, then the dividend yield is

   A 2.0

   B $2

   C 12.5%

   D 8%

17 **[HL Only]**   Which of the statements below is true given the following information: dividends per share $0.35, earnings per share $0.50, and current market price of share $12.

   A Dividend yield is $0.35 per share

   B Retained profit is $0.15 per share

   C The share is overvalued at $12 per share

   D Shareholders receive $0.50 per share held

18 **[HL Only]**   The dividend yield ratio shows

   A The dividend per share expressed as a percentage of the current share price

   B The earnings per share as a percentage of total dividend payments

   C The maximum dividends that can be paid to shareholders

   D How much return shareholders get from investing in a company

19 **[HL Only]**   Which statement below *cannot* be applied to the dividend yield ratio?

   A The amount of dividends received as a percentage of the market price of the share

   B Calculated by dividends divided by market price of share, expressed as a percentage

   C If the market price increases, then the yield tends to be lower

   D Investors use this ratio to compare the returns to those of other investment opportunities

20 The gearing ratio measures

    A The amount of long-term finance of a firm

    B The size of creditors in relation to a firm's capital employed

    C The proportion of the a firm's capital employed formed by interest-bearing debt

    D The borrowing of a firm as a percentage of its total assets

21 Which statement below *cannot* be applied to the gearing ratio?

    A It looks at the amount of external sources of finances

    B It is a long-term liquidity ratio

    C Creditors prefer firms to have high gearing as it means they make more profit

    D Firms with a high gearing ratio are generally considered to be a risky investment

22 Gearing can be calculated as

    A Loan capital plus other borrowings expressed as a proportion of capital employed

    B Net Assets divided by Long-term Liabilities

    C External sources of funds as a percentage of Total Assets Employed

    D Liabilities as a percentage of capital employed

23 Banks and other lenders would be least interested in looking at which financial ratio?

    A Return on capital employed

    B Acid test

    C Earnings per share

    D Gearing

24 Which question can ratio analysis *not* address?

    A How does the firm's performance compare to it nearest rivals?

    B Is the firm profitable?

    C Can the firm pay its liabilities?

    D Has the firm's market share improved?

25 **[HL Only]**   The formula for earnings per share is

    A Net profit after tax divided by number of ordinary shares

    B Net profit before tax divided by number of ordinary shares

    C Dividends paid divided by sales revenue

    D Sales revenue divided by Capital Employed

26 **[HL Only]**   The formula for dividend yield is

    A Dividends expressed as a percentage of Capital Employed

    B Dividends expressed as a percentage of Sales Revenue

    C Dividends per share as a percentage of the market price of each share

    D Dividends per share as a percentage of net profit after tax and interest

27 The gearing ratio can be expressed as

    A (Liabilities / Capital Employed) * 100

    B (Long-term liabilities / Equity plus Long-term liabilities) * 100

    C Short-term liabilities plus Long-term liabilities expressed as a percentage of the Capital Employed

    D Long-term liabilities expressed as a percentage of Sales Revenue

28 Which of the following sources of finance will raise the value of the gearing ratio?

   A Debentures

   B Initial public offering

   C Debt factoring

   D Bank overdraft

29 It is generally desirable for a firm to have a relatively low value for which of its financial ratios?

   A ROCE

   B Stock turnover

   C GPM

   D Debtor days

30 All the following are reasons for conducting financial ratio analysis, except for which option?

   A To improve organizational accountability

   B To aid management decision making and control

   C Assessing the value of profit over time

   D Best practice benchmarking

31 **[HL Only]**   The debtor days ratio shows

   A The credit sales made as a percentage of sales turnover

   B The amount of debtors as a percentage of sales turnover

   C How long, on average, it takes a firm to pay it debts to its suppliers and creditors

   D How long, on average, it takes a firm to collect its debts from its customers

32 **[HL Only]**   The creditor days ratio shows

   A The credit sales made as a percentage of sales turnover

   B The amount of creditors as a percentage of sales turnover

   C How long, on average, it takes a firm to pay it debts to its suppliers and creditors

   D How long, on average, it takes a firm to collect its debts from its customers

33 **[HL Only]**   A business is most likely to prefer a …….. debt collection period with a ……….. creditor days ratio

   A short, large

   B long, short

   C short, short

   D long, large

34 **[HL Only]**   If a business has sold stock valued at a cost of $150,000 (the cost of sales) and has $25,000 owed to trade creditors, what is the ratio for creditor days?

   A 6 days

   B 17 days

   C 61 days

   D 83 days

35 **[HL Only]**   Suppose Argueta Ltd. has sales revenues of $150,000, cost of sales valued at $70,000 and debtors to the value of $30,000. Calculate the average debt collection period for the firm.

   A 27 days

   B 73 days

   C 97 days

   D 243 days

UNIT

4

Unit 4.1   The Role of Marketing

Task 1: Complete the missing words

Marketing is about the identification, anticipation and .... of the needs of customers, whilst making a .... Firms without much competition tend to be more product-focused (known as .... orientation). A market-led business has its focus on the needs and requirements of the ....

Task 2: Explain ...

a   How businesses might calculate their market share

_____

_____

_____

_____

b   One advantage and one disadvantage to a business that plans to launch new products in rapidly growing markets

_____

_____

_____

_____

c   The difference between commercial marketing and social marketing, using the costs and benefits of smoking as an example

_____

_____

_____

_____

Task 3: True or false?

		True / False
a	Marketing is concerned with promoting goods and services to consumers.	
b	Marketing is the same as advertising and selling.	
c	Markets can exist without physical locations.	
d	The marketing mix is a central feature of any marketing plan.	
e	Advertising is what gets a product sold.	
f	Consumer markets are the products directly aimed at individuals and households.	

Task 4: Vocabulary quiz

Identify the key terms from the clues given. *Hint*: the answers are in *reverse* alphabetical order.

Key Term	Definition
	The marketing approach that does not respond well to change because the needs of customers and the market are not catered for.
	A document outlining the marketing mix of an organization in order to achieve its marketing objectives.
	Usually measured by calculating the sales of a firm as a percentage of all sales in the market.
	A marketing or decision-making approach that places the customer as the key to success.

Task 5: Calculating market share

a   Complete the missing figures in the table below for a market valued at $150 million.

Company	Sales ($m)	Market share (%)
A	60	
B	30	
C		22
D		18

b   Based on your answers to the above, calculate and comment on the two firm concentration ratio.

_____

_____

Task 6: Multiple choice

1   The size of a market cannot be measured in terms of

   A   Sales revenue

   B   Sales volume

   C   Number of customers

   D   Marketing budgets

2   Which of the following is *not* part of the marketing mix for the marketing of goods?

   A   Product

   B   Promotion

   C   People

   D   Place

3   The marketing mix for services does *not* include

   A   Price

   B   Physical environment

   C   Pledge

   D   People

4   Marketing is about all the following things except

  A Understanding the needs and wants of customers

  B Meeting the needs and wants of customers

  C Customer relations

  D Recruiting the best sales people

5   One difference between goods and services is that services are

  A Perishable

  B Owned upon purchase

  C Tangible

  D Homogeneous

6   Market orientation is a marketing strategy that involves

  A Researching consumers' needs in order to develop new products

  B Producing innovative goods that meet the needs of the market

  C Developing products based on a firm's production capability

  D Primary research techniques to find out about customers' wants and needs

7   Which statement cannot be applied to the nature of marketing?

  A Customers are of central importance to marketing

  B Marketing affects all parts of a business

  C Marketing is all about selling to meet the needs of customers

  D Marketing is not the same as advertising

8   A marketing plan is least likely to include

  A A SWOT analysis

  B Marketing objectives

  C Financial information

  D Methods of production

9   Market share can be described as

  A The total sales, as measured by value or volume, in a market

  B The percentage of total sales in a market that can be attributed to a firm

  C The number of suppliers in the market

  D The relative size of a market

10 Which statement cannot be applied to *market orientated* businesses?

  A Products are produced that customers actually want or need

  B Prices take account of what people are prepared and able to pay

  C There is heavy spending on product research and development

  D Customer buying habits enable a firm to establish promotional strategies

11 The physical element in the marketing of a service is known as the

  A Product

  B Physical environment

  C Ambience

  D Feel-good factor

12 An advantage of higher market share is that

   A It can lead to market leadership or dominance

   B It requires economies of scale to be earned

   C There will be less competitors in the market

   D The firm will operate more productively

13 Product orientated marketing means

   A Using a firm's strengths such as its brand image to market existing and new products

   B Marketing decisions based on the needs of customers

   C Producing and marketing products that the firm believes will sell

   D Using a firm's assets to increase the marketing budget

14 The marketing approach that uses the strengths of a business to market both new and existing products is known as

   A Product orientation

   B Market orientation

   C Asset-led marketing

   D Social marketing

15 Core competencies of a business are unlikely to include its

   A Brand names

   B Global reach

   C Distribution channels

   D Newly recruited staff

16 Organizations trying to market healthier diets and eating habits are most likely to use

   A Asset-led marketing

   B Social marketing

   C Product orientation

   D Market orientation

17 Which feature cannot be applied to market orientated businesses?

   A Research is conducted on the needs and wants of customers

   B Products are designed according to what the producer feels will sell the best

   C Price is based on the ability and willingness of customers to pay

   D Distribution networks make it convenient for customers to make purchases

18 Which of the following is an example of a marketing objective for Toys R Us?

   A Increase output by 1 million toys by the end of this year

   B Open 5 new stores in Vietnam within the next three years

   C Increase market share by 5% within the next 20 months

   D Increase brand awareness through above-the-line promotions

19 Hannah has decided to open a franchise of Le Café Ltd in a busy commercial district. She has decided to employ premium pricing for its range of coffees and desserts. She has decided to advertise by distributing flyers and coupons in the local area.

Which elements of the marketing mix below have not been mentioned for the above situation?

A Price, Promotion and People

B Place, Physical environment and Profit

C Place, Price, Promotion

D People, Physical environment, Process

20 Identify an alternative marketing approach to market orientation from the given options.

A Service orientation

B Consumer orientation

C Production orientation

D Product orientation

21 Marketing that exploits the strengths of a business, such as its brand name, to market both new and existing products is known as

A Asset-led marketing

B Market-led marketing

C Consumer-led marketing

D Product-led marketing

22 Which of the following is *not* part of the marketing mix for services?

A Customer relations management

B Pricing

C Production

D Distribution

23 Marketing that takes account of the moral issues involved in business is known as

A E-marketing

B Persuasive marketing

C Ethical marketing

D Advocacy marketing

24 The management of an organization's relations and interactions with its customers is known as

A Human resources management

B Human relations management

C Customer relations management

D Public relations management

25 Some businesses are seen to have senior managers chauffeured in expensive cars, partly to portray an image of high quality and standards. This is an example of

A Packaging

B People management

C Process management

D Physical evidence

Unit 4.2   Marketing Planning

Task 1: Vocabulary quiz

Identify the key terms from the clues given. *Hint*: the answers are in alphabetical order.

Key Term	Definition
	Marketing activities designed to discover the opinions, beliefs and feelings of potential and existing customers.
	A particular customer group within a market for a product which has shared characteristics and needs that are targeted by marketers.
	The approach taken by an organization in order to achieve its marketing objectives.
	The term used to describe the total number of people in a market.
	A popular analytic tool that looks at the determinants of the intensity of competition in an industry: Buyers, Suppliers, Substitutes, New Entrants and Rivalry.
	A technique that shows how a product is perceived in relation to other products or brands that are available in the same market.
	The most common form of primary research that uses a series of questions in order to collect data from a representative sample.
	The practice of selecting a small group or segment of a population for a particular market for market research purposes.
	A statistical technique that identifies trends in historical data, often adjusted for seasonal and cyclical fluctuations. This information can then be used to make extrapolations.
	Refers to an exclusive customer benefit that no other organization can claim for its product.

Task 2: True or false?

		True / False
a	Desk research involves collecting new data that is in a useable format for a firm.	
b	Field research tends to be relatively cheaper to collect and collate than desk research.	
c	Market research can reduce risk in business decision-making because it provides better information to managers.	
d	Prices in niche markets tend to be relatively low due to the amount of competition that exists.	
e	Questionnaires can be used to collect qualitative and quantitative data.	
f	Niche markets are those which provide goods and services that appeal to an extensive number of customers.	
g	Striving for increased market share would be an example of a marketing objective.	

| h | Skilled interviewers are required to conduct qualitative research which can be expensive as they have to be paid for their time and expertise. | |
| i | Sampling is used to conduct primary research and it is used because asking every person in a population to respond to a survey would be too time consuming and costly. | |

Task 3: Sampling   [Higher Level Extension]

Identify the sampling method from the clues given.

	Sampling Method
Sampling a given number of people who share similar characteristics, such as teenagers or divorced parents about their summer holidays.	
Method where everyone has an equal chance of being selected for sampling.	
An appropriate sample, based on different market segments, is chosen to represent the views of the population.	
Dividing the population into geographical areas and taking certain regions as the sample.	

Task 4: Explain the difference between ...

a   Qualitative market research and Quantitative market research

_____

_____

b   Market segments and Market segmentation

_____

_____

c   Ad hoc market research and Continuous market research

_____

_____

d   Market share and Monopoly, as was stated by Microsoft CEO Steve Balimer who said, "We don't have a monopoly. We have market share. There's a difference."

_____

_____

e   Niche marketing and Mass marketing

_____

_____

Task 5: Multiple choice – Market research

1 Which of the following is *not* a potential problem associated with primary research data?

   A Sample size

   B Bias

   C Focus

   D Cost

2 Primary research is

   A Data that has not been processed by a firm

   B Using questionnaires to collect quantitative data

   C Collecting new data for a specific purpose

   D Using experimentation and observations to find out what customers want or need

3 Why might a business carry out primary research?

   A To gather data required that does not already exist

   B To discover their customers' needs and wants

   C To produce better goods or services for their customers

   D To gain more market share

4 Which of the following is *not* a source of secondary data?

   A Reference books

   B Government publications

   C Observations

   D Company annual reports

5 Primary data has an advantage over secondary data because

   A The data already exists so is cheaper to gather

   B It is normally less time consuming to gather

   C It saves data collection time

   D It is unique to the purpose of the research

6 The difference between quantitative and qualitative market research is that

   A The latter method relies on a much larger number of respondents to get a statistically valid set of answers

   B The former method uses a large sample size

   C One relies on primary research whilst the other relies on secondary research

   D The former method can be statistically analysed

7 The main purpose of a researcher using qualitative market research is to

   A Understand the behaviour, attitudes and perceptions of customers or employees

   B Aid marketing or organizational decision-making

   C Aid statistical analysis of factual findings

   D Gather the views of a small group of people before the mass launch of a product

8 Which statement below cannot be applied to quantitative market research?

   A Uses hard data and facts to aid statistical analyses

   B Is based on numerical data and information

   C Is based on only using primary research techniques

   D Deals with questions such as 'how much', 'how many' and 'how often'

9 Which of the following is an example of primary research?

   A Newly published government reports

   B Customer suggestion or comment sheets

   C Economic forecasts for the next twelve months

   D Information from competitors

10 Secondary data can be gathered from the use of

   A Focus groups

   B Observations

   C Suggestion boxes

   D Social trends

11 Primary data can be gathered from the use of

   A Government statistics

   B Internet sites

   C Group interviews

   D Economic forecasts

12 Which of the following is unlikely to be a drawback of primary research?

   A Unrepresentative sample used to generate findings

   B Respondents may exaggerate their views

   C Wrong or inappropriate questions may be asked

   D May lack specific focus

13 Primary research can be obtained by several methods except for

   A Observations

   B Focus groups

   C University research publications

   D Photographic evidence

14 Market research is *not* concerned with

   A Trying to identify market trends

   B Assessing consumer reactions to a new product

   C Forecasting potential sales of a new product

   D Segmenting markets by age, gender, income and ethnic background

15 Primary data is .... research that collects .... data for a specific purpose.

   A Desk, existing

   B New, new

   C Field, new

   D Field, existing

16 Desk research can be conducted by
  A Personal interviews
  B Telephone interviews
  C Postal surveys
  D Using company annual accounts

17 Primary data can be best gathered by
  A Government publications and statistics
  B Observation and surveillance
  C Quantitative research
  D Trade research and development

18 Market research that gathers the opinions, ideas, views and thoughts of consumers in a non-statistical manner is known as
  A Primary research
  B Desk research
  C Qualitative research
  D Quantitative research

19 Market research that gathers statistical data is known as
  A Field research
  B Secondary research
  C Qualitative research
  D Quantitative research

20 Which statement below cannot be applied to desk research?
  A It uses existing data and information for market research purposes
  B Data is often provided by specialist market research firms
  C It includes the use of survey and interview findings conducted by the firm
  D It includes industry surveys that have been carried out

Task 6: Multiple choice – Market segmentation, consumer profiles and market mapping

1 The study of human population dynamics is known as
  A Segmentation
  B Demography
  C Geography
  D Psychology

2 Demographic segmentation can be done by all the following except
  A Gender
  B Age
  C Lifestyle
  D Religion

3   Which statement below cannot be applied to market segmentation?

   A It acknowledges the fact that customers are different

   B It is used for primary research only

   C Demographics is the most common method of segmentation

   D It allows a firm to fine-tune its marketing mix

4   If a firm uses a segmentation strategy based on characteristics such as religion, gender and marital status, then it is using which type of segmentation?

   A Demographic

   B Geographic

   C Psychographic

   D Ethnicity

5   The image or perception of a product or brand in relation to other products or brands in the market is known as

   A Positioning

   B Branding

   C Segmentation

   D Physical evidence

6   Businesses that view their customers as being the same and therefore offer just one marketing mix take a .... approach to their marketing.

   A Targeting

   B Segmentation

   C Homogeneous

   D Heterogeneous

7   A product's location on a position map is determined by the

   A Producers

   B Consumers

   C Competitors

   D Suppliers

8   A 'cowboy brand' is likely to be perceived as one that offers

   A High quality at high price

   B Low quality at high price

   C High quality at low price

   D Low quality at low price

9   A 'premium brand' is likely to be perceived as one that offers

   A High quality at high price

   B Low quality at high price

   C High quality at low price

   D Low quality at low price

10 McDonald's introduced salads to its menu to target the more health-aware customer. This is an example of which type of segmentation?

A Demographic

B Geographic

C Psychographic

D Prolific

11 The strategy that involves changing the perception of a product or brand relative to those offered by rival firms is known as

A Market mapping

B Perceptual mapping

C Remapping

D Repositioning

12 Segmentation can be split into three broad categories. Which option below is *not* one of the methods?

A Academics

B Demographics

C Geographic

D Psychographics

13 The name for a collective group of people who have the same needs and wants for a particular product is known as a

A Consumer group

B Market

C Market division

D Target audience

14 If Audi is perceived as being inferior to rivals BMW and Mercedes, then the firm needs to review its

A Segmentation

B Positioning

C Demographics

D Corporate image

15 Which concept refers to any distinctive aspect or feature of a product that differentiates it from others that might be available on the market?

A Competitive rivalry

B Monopolistic power

C Unique selling point

D Corporate branding

Task 7: Multiple choice – Sampling methods [Higher Level Extension]

1   Sampling is used in market research because

    A   It is cheaper and quicker to use a sample than to survey the whole market

    B   A sample's views is used to represent the population's views

    C   A sample can be used to increase the confidence level of statistical findings

    D   It can be easier to identify trends from the sample findings

2   The sampling method used to interview a given number of respondents with given characteristics, such as their age and gender, is known as

    A   Cluster

    B   Random

    C   Stratified

    D   Quota

3   Which method of sampling gives each member of the public an equal chance of being selected as part of a sample?

    A   Cluster

    B   Random

    C   Stratified

    D   Quota

4   Which method of sampling is used when a population is widely dispersed across geographical locations?

    A   Cluster

    B   Random

    C   Stratified

    D   Quota

5   Which of the following is *not* a feature of quota sampling?

    A   Non-randomly selected sample

    B   Specific number of people in a market segment is selected

    C   Likely to be very representative of the population

    D   Relatively cheap to select the sample

6   Stratified sampling would be least likely to take account of

    A   Race or ethnicity

    B   Occupations

    C   Heterogeneous characteristics of a population

    D   Homogenous characteristics of a population

7   Snowballing is

    A   Primary research that builds on the work conducted by secondary researchers

    B   Secondary research that stems from the work of primary researchers

    C   Surveys or interviews carried out with individuals, who then suggest other friends, family or colleagues to increase the sample

    D   Secondary research that mounts very quickly due to the vast amount of information that is available

8 Which of the following is *not* a source of sampling error?

   A Small sample size

   B Bias

   C Dishonesty

   D Errors made in recording data

9 Segmentation can bring about potential advantages except

   A Risk spreading

   B Easier to identify and select appropriate advertising media

   C Less waste due to focused marketing

   D The time involved in compiling customer profiles for market segmentation

10 Which category of segmentation is least likely to be used by a private fee-paying school?

   A Socio-economic grouping

   B Age

   C Geographical location

   D Ethnicity and religion

11 Sampling errors are likely to occur if

   A The sample size is significantly large

   B A representative sample is selected

   C Random sampling is used

   D There are sampling discrepancies

12 Research carried out via in-depth interviews in order to determine the reasons behind consumers' attitudes and opinions is best described as

   A Quantitative research

   B Qualitative research

   C Secondary research

   D Market research

13 Market research data and information which is collected from other sources is known as

   A Desk research

   B Field research

   C Primary research

   D Quantitative research

14 Porter's five forces do *not* include

   A Intensity of rivalry

   B Power of suppliers

   C Substitutes in the industry

   D Market growth potential

15 Porter described the 'threat of substitutes' in an industry as

   A The ability of customers to switch to an alternative product or brand

   B The existence of substitute products within a market

   C The number of existing products and brands in an industry

   D The degree of customer loyalty to a brand or product

16 The sampling method that allows each entity in a population to have an equal chance of being in the sample is known as

    A Snowballing

    B Random sampling

    C Quota sampling

    D Stratified sampling

17 The sampling method that relies on word of mouth to get relevant subjects (people) for a sample is known as

    A Snowballing

    B Random sampling

    C Quota sampling

    D Stratified sampling

18 The sampling methods that involves interviewing people according to a common characteristic or attribute from a specific subgroup of a population is known as

    A Snowballing

    B Random sampling

    C Quota sampling

    D Stratified sampling

19 What is the name given to the process of gathering, recording and analysing data relating to a good or service in order to make more informed marketing decisions?

    A Marketing planning

    B Market segmentation

    C Market research

    D Market mapping

20 The name given to a representative group of a population (every person in a particular market) being used for market research purposes is a

    A Target market

    B Demographic group

    C Sample

    D Segment

Unit 4.3   Product

Task 1: Vocabulary quiz

Identify the key terms from the clues given. *Hint*: the answers are in alphabetical order.

Key Term	Definition
	A name given by an organization to its product or service with the aim of making the name stand out from those of rivals.
	A situation where customers buy their preferred brand of a particular product and they are reluctant to switch to another brand.
	Long-lasting products purchased by individuals for personal use, such as cars, furniture, games consoles and washing machines.
	Goods and services that are made distinctive from products of rival firms.
	Methods used to lengthen the product life cycle of a particular product.
	A unique graphical representation (such as a symbol, font or picture) of a business or its brand.
	The stage in the product life cycle when sales are at, or near, their maximum and there is little scope for any growth.
	A marketing strategy that tries to give a product a unique element so that it stands out from other products.
	Marketing theory that depicts the phases a typical product goes through during its commercial existence.
	A part (or unit) of a business that has separate aims and objectives and can be planned, managed and organized independently of other firms owned by the business.

Task 2: True or false?

		True / False
a	The term 'products' refers to physical goods rather than services.	
b	Most of the new products launched by well-known multinationals are successful.	
c	Rapid changes in technology and fashion trends have shortened the life cycles of products in certain industries.	
d	Brands are more likely to succeed than to fail.	
e	Brand leaders are the most popular brands in the view of the public.	
f	M&M's chocolates are made by Mars. M&M's is therefore a brand label of the Mars company.	

Task 3: Identify the company

Identify the company from its given brands and registered trademarks. *Hint*: think about 'Brands'....

Company	Industry	Brands and Trademarks
	Automobiles	M3, M5, M6, X5, Z4, Mini
	Cosmetics	Fire & Ice, Flex, Ultima, Eterna, Charlie
	Electronics	QuickTime, Mac OS X, Macintosh, iPod
	Confectionary	Kit Kat, Smarties, Nescafe, Perrier, Nestea, Dreyer's
	Luxury fashion	CD, Fahrenheit, Dune, Poison
	Electronics	Cybershot, PlayStation, PSP, Walkman

Task 4: Product portfolio analysis

a   Products that have low market share in a high growth market are known as question marks. True or false?

b   The Boston Matrix can be used to assess the portfolio of strategic business units for a company. True or false?

c   Assuming that Stars, in the Boston Matrix, maintain their relative market share they will eventually become cash cows.   True or false?

d   The Boston Matrix could be useful for a business trying to manage a diverse range of products in its portfolio.   True or false?

e   Product portfolio management is the responsibility of all managers in an organization. True or false?

f   What is the name given to the category of products in the Boston Matrix that has high or rising market share within a growing market?   ....

g   Portfolio management is not used to achieve which goal?
   i   Maximize the profitability of the portfolio
   ii   Provide balance in a firm's portfolio
   iii   Determine customer perceptions of the portfolio
   iv   Support the corporate strategy

h   Products that have suffered from relatively inferior marketing or product quality are known as
   i   Wild cards
   ii   Dogs
   iii   Cash Cows
   iv   Stars

i   According to the Boston Consultancy Group, a firm that has too many ..... will suffer from poor .....
   i   Problem children, Cash flow
   ii   Dogs, Cash flow
   iii   Dogs, Profit
   iv   Question marks, Profit

j   Match the product category with its stage in the product life cycle.

A	Cash cows	Z	Decline
B	Dogs	Y	Growth
C	Stars	X	Launch
D	Wild cards	W	Maturity

Task 5: Multiple choice

1   Products that are sold from one business to another to further the production process are known as
   A Durable goods
   B Perishable goods
   C Capital goods
   D Consumer goods

2   Non-durable products, such as fresh ice cream, are also known as
   A Consumer products
   B Convenience products
   C Perishables
   D Speciality goods

3   A brand cannot be represented by which of the following?
   A A symbol
   B A logo
   C Packaging
   D A product

4   Pre-launch activities do *not* include
   A Generating ideas
   B Market research
   C Perception mapping
   D Test marketing

5   A group or variety of products that serves the same purpose in a particular market is known as a
   A Product line
   B Product mix
   C Product range
   D Product portfolio

6   McDonald's variety of value meals is an example of its
   A Product line
   B Product mix
   C Product range
   D Product portfolio

7 The marketing strategy used to give products a unique aspect so that customers can distinguish between the product and those offered by other firms is known as

   A Product orientation

   B Product differentiation

   C Unique selling point

   D Product range

8 Possible strategies to reverse the decline in sales of a product do *not* include

   A Expanding into new markets overseas

   B Increasing prices to improve the image of the product

   C Increased use of promotional strategies

   D Additional features added to the product, such as special or limited editions

9 Which of the following is a possible reason for an increase in the sales of a product?

   A Newer and better alternatives become available on the market

   B A smaller channel of distribution

   C Lower prices for products with few substitutes

   D Redesigned packaging to increase the emotional value of the product

10 Which of the following is *not* an extension strategy?

   A Reducing prices to attract more customers

   B Advertising used to remind and entice customers to make a purchase

   C Producing new products to sell abroad

   D Exporting to overseas markets

11 Which feature does *not* necessarily apply to fast-moving consumer goods (FMCGs)?

   A Products that sell in high volumes

   B Products that have low profit margins

   C Rely on consumer repurchase

   D Products that are not durable

12 Brand image is the ………. that customers have about a particular brand. A strong brand image will lead to demand for the product being more price ……….

   A Culture, Elastic

   B Culture, Inelastic

   C Perception, Inelastic

   D Perception, Elastic

13 Which of the following is *not* part of new product development?

   A Test marketing

   B Research and development

   C Market research

   D Extension strategies

14 Which of the items below is unlikely to be considered as a HIP (high involvement product)?

   A Private boarding school education

   B Family vacation to both America and Canada

   C Vintage wine

   D Birthday cards

15 The technique of using an existing brand name to launch a new or modified product is known as
  A Brand extension
  B Branding
  C Repositioning
  D Differentiation

16 Which of the following would most likely be classed as a perishable consumer product?
  A Motor vehicle
  B Fridge freezer
  C Fresh food
  D Toys

17 White goods (a type of consumer durable) do *not* include
  A Washing machines
  B Cookers
  C Microwaves
  D Games consoles

18 The strategy of using a well-established trademark to develop and sell new products is called
  A Brand loyalty
  B Brand extension
  C Product differentiation
  D Extension strategy

19 The stage in a product's life cycle that requires significant investment yet will often incur losses is known as
  A Launch
  B Growth
  C Saturation
  D Decline

20 The objective of new product development is *least* likely to include
  A To increase sales turnover
  B To increase market share
  C To gain a competitive edge
  D To raise brand awareness

21 Products that have a high market share in a high growth market are known as
  A Stars
  B Cash cows
  C Dogs
  D Wild cards

22 Products that have high market share in a low growth market are known as
  A Dogs
  B Cash cows
  C Stars
  D Problem children

23 'Laggards' are purchasers in which stage of a product's life cycle?

  A Maturity

  B Decline

  C Growth

  D Launch

24 'Decline' is

  A The last stage of a product's life cycle, when sales fall sharply

  B A fall in the output of the economy

  C A fall in sales revenue

  D When sales fall faster than costs of production

25 Convenience products that are sold in retail outlets on a daily basis are known as

  A White goods

  B Fast-moving consumer goods

  C Soft goods

  D High involvement products

26 The term used to describe a variety of the same product that a business produces is the

  A Product mix

  B Product portfolio

  C Product line

  D Product range

27 Products that require little thought, effort and expense are known as

  A Consumer goods

  B Durable goods

  C Convenience goods

  D Shopping goods

28 Speciality goods include all the following except

  A Sports cars

  B Gourmet food

  C Jewellery

  D IB Science textbooks

29 Which of the following activities does *not* take place during the research and development stage of the product life cycle?

  A Market research

  B Monitoring of competitors

  C Test marketing

  D Publicity

30 Features of the 'launch' stage of a product's life cycle exclude

  A Low sales volume

  B Extensive promotion and advertising

  C Negative cash flow for most products

  D Market research

31 [HL Only]   Which statement does *not* refer to a role or function of branding?

  A It gives a unique character or association to a product

  B It encourages repeat custom and customer loyalty

  C It allows firms to charge above-average prices

  D It allows firms to charge lower prices to attract more sales

32 [HL Only]   What is the name given to a product that has the largest market share in a particular industry?

  A Brand leader

  B Brand loyalty

  C Glocalized brand

  D Brand development

33 [HL Only]   Brands such as Gucci, Tiffany & Co and Rolls Royce are perceived as being high in quality and high in price. These brands are therefore known as

  A Economy brands

  B Premium brands

  C Value brands

  D Rip-off brands

34 [HL Only]   Which of the following is an example of an own-label brand?

  A Rolex watch

  B Wal-Mart white wine

  C Samsung Anycall mobile phone

  D Doritos tortilla potato chips

35 [HL Only]   A brand that is owned by the producer of a product is known as

  A Producer's brand

  B Manufacturer's brand

  C Private label brand

  D Copyright

36 [HL Only]   The strategy of using a unified brand name, in order to build customer loyalty and trust, for a range of products offered by a firm is known as

  A Family branding

  B Corporate branding

  C Own-label branding

  D Manufacturer's branding

37 [HL Only]   Which type of branding can best benefit from economies of scope in advertising?

  A Individual

  B Umbrella

  C Corporate

  D Own-label

38 [HL Only]   Features of a good brand name do not tend to include the name being

A Easy enough to pronounce and spell

B Memorable

C Distinctive/unique

D Associated with the mission of the business

39 [HL Only]   When customers are reluctant to switch away from purchasing their favourite brand of a particular product, this is known as

A Brand dependability

B Brand loyalty

C Brand fidelity

D Brand development

40 [HL Only]   When an organization becomes complacent about their product strategy and fails to keep up with market changes, this is known as

A Gratification

B Marketing myopia

C Short-termism

D Portfolio negligence

Unit 4.4   Price

Task 1: Vocabulary quiz – Pricing strategies

Identify the key terms from the clues given. *Hint*: the answers are in *reverse* alphabetical order.

Key Term	Definition
	Setting a high price and only gradually reduce prices as competitors enter the market.
	Setting prices to make them seem (at least slightly) lower, such as $9.95 rather than $10.00.
	Pricing strategy used by firms with the largest market share in an industry, with other smaller firms following the price set by the market leaders.
	Charging different prices to different market segments for essentially the same product, such as peak and off-peak transportation or child and adult fares.
	Charging a very low price, perhaps below costs, to damage the sales of competitors.
	Setting a very low price in order to gain access into a market.
	Setting prices based on the prices set by rival businesses.
	Adding a fixed amount or percentage to costs of production to determine the selling price.

Task 2: Explain why ...

a   First class airline travel is not an example of price discrimination

_____

_____

b   Firms are usually more willing to produce and sell more of their products at a higher price

_____

_____

c   [HL Only]   Knowledge of price elasticity of demand may be useful for a business

_____

_____

d   [HL Only]   The price elasticity of demand for organic food is likely to be relatively price inelastic

_____

_____

e   Prestige pricing differs from Price skimming

_____

_____

Task 3: True or false?

		True / False
a	An increase in supply will, other things being constant, result in a fall in the price of a product.	
b	Price skimming tends to be used for fast-moving consumer goods.	
c	In theory, if the consumer could buy direct from the manufacturer then the price of the product would be lower.	
d	[HL Only] Effective promotion can help to make the demand for a product more price inelastic.	
e	[HL Only] The cross price elasticity of demand for two goods in competitive demand, i.e. substitutes, is positive.	
f	[HL Only] Knowledge of the income elasticity of demand for different products can help businesses to forecast sales.	
g	[HL Only] A product is likely to have a high price elasticity of demand if there is high consumer and brand loyalty for the product.	
h	The price decision will influence the customer's view of a product's quality.	

Task 4: Odd one out [Higher Level Extension]

Select the odd one out from each of the options below.

a	Skimming	Loss leader	Penetration	Predatory
b	Price leadership	Predatory	Going rate	Psychological
c	Income	Price	Fashion and tastes	Price of substitutes
d	Costs of production	Consumer incomes	Corporation tax	Government subsidies

Task 5: Calculating elasticity of demand [Higher Level Extension]

a   The price of a bottle of wine falls from $30 to $25, resulting in an increase in demand from 95 bottles to 114 bottles per day. Calculate the PED and comment on the result.

_____

_____

_____

b   Apply the theory of Income Elasticity of Demand to classify the following products into either normal goods (necessities or luxuries) or inferior goods by marking the correct boxes.

	Normal	Inferior		Normal	Inferior
Canned fruits and vegetables			Rolex watches		
Casual clothing			Single-ply tissue paper		
Christian Dior perfume			Supermarket own-brands		
Fresh fruits and vegetables			Tiffany & Co jewellery		

c The price of coffee increases from $4.50 to $4.95 per jar and it is observed in the subsequent time period that the quantity demanded for tea rises from 200 boxes to 225 boxes per week. Calculate the cross price elasticity of demand and comment on your findings.

_____

_____

_____

_____

d Explain what is wrong (i.e. not strictly correct) with each of the following statements.

i "The price is sensitive to demand."

_____

_____

ii "Price elastic means as price goes up, so demand falls."

_____

_____

iii "Demand must be income elastic because as the price dropped, demand rose."

_____

_____

iv "An airline company could raise sales revenues by using loss leader pricing."

_____

_____

Task 6: Multiple choice – Pricing strategies

1 Pricing strategies that are based on the prices set relative to a rival's price are known as
  A Cost-based pricing
  B Competitor pricing
  C Price taker
  D Price setter

2 Firms that operate in highly competitive markets and do not, therefore, have any price setting power are known as
  A Price setters
  B Price makers
  C Price takers
  D Price laggers

3 **[HL Only]** Which factor could best account for the increase in sales revenue growth for a business?
  A Higher intensity of competition in the market
  B Higher prices for price-inelastic products
  C Low advertising elasticity of demand
  D Lower prices for price-inelastic products

4   Identify the factor that does *not* directly affect the demand for Chan & Cahill Financial Services.

    A Consumer confidence levels in stock and financial markets

    B Income levels of customers

    C The fee of using their financial services

    D A change in qualifications needed to work in financial services

5   Which of the following prices is the best example of psychological pricing?

    A $9.95

    B $8.50

    C $1.00

    D $0.25

Questions 6–8 relate to the information given in the following table.

Cost of Raw Materials for A1 Bakery in June

Flour	$10,600
Whipped cream	$12,000
Fresh fruits	$25,000
Output	11,900

6   Given the limited information, what is the break-even price?

    A $3

    B $4

    C $5

    D $6

7   Which of the following prices is *not* an example of cost-based pricing for A1 Bakery?

    A $3.95

    B $4.00

    C $4.50

    D $4.95

8   If the price is set at $6, then the mark-up per unit would be

    A $1

    B $4

    C 20%

    D 50%

9   Which statement cannot be applied to penetration pricing policies?

    A Used when there are existing rivals

    B Aims to establish higher market share

    C Involves setting a relatively low price

    D Prices set according to the average price level

10 When the same product, usually a service, is sold in different markets for different prices, this is known as

  A Price skimming

  B Penetration pricing

  C Price discrimination

  D Destroyer pricing

11 Which short-term pricing strategy can be used by a firm that is potentially threatened by the entry of a new supplier?

  A Price skimming

  B Price discrimination

  C Predatory pricing

  D Penetration pricing

12 One purpose of using price skimming is to

  A Maximize long-term sales revenue

  B Maximize short-term profit margins

  C Prevent other firms from entering the market

  D Enter a market new

13 Using prices of similar goods as a guide to setting the price for a product is called

  A Competitive pricing

  B Predatory pricing

  C Cost-based pricing

  D Contribution based pricing

14 The strategy of setting a permanently high price for a luxury product that has high kudos is called

  A Skimming price

  B Prestige pricing

  C Price leadership

  D Premium pricing

15 When might a business be most likely to use price skimming?

  A In order to establish greater market share

  B When it is the market leader in the industry

  C To eliminate smaller rivals from the market

  D To introduce an original and unique product

16 **[HL Only]**   The pricing strategy that involves a firm setting prices so low that smaller competitors are forced out of the market is known as

  A Market penetration

  B Market destruction

  C Predatory pricing

  D Price leadership

17 **[HL Only]**   Supermarkets and other retailers often sell their own-brand products at a loss in order to entice sales of other more profitable products. Such a strategy is known as

   A Price leadership

   B Loss leader pricing

   C Pre-emptive pricing

   D Price discrimination

18 **[HL Only]**   .... occurs when a firm charges different prices to different groups of customers for essentially the same product.

   A Price discrimination

   B Differentiation

   C Pre-emptive pricing

   D Price leadership

19 **[HL Only]**   Alison & Marshall Foods Ltd increases the price of its fruit baskets from \$5 to \$6. As a result, it sees a drop in demand from 100 to 90 fruit baskets a week. What is the value of the price elasticity of demand for the product?

   A 2.0

   B 1.5

   C 0.5

   D 1.0

20 **[HL Only]**   Other things being equal, an increase in demand will result in

   A An increase in the cost of the product

   B A fall in the price of the product

   C An increase in the price and a rise in the quantity traded

   D An increase in the price and a fall in the quantity traded

Task 7: Multiple choice – Demand, supply and elasticity [Higher Level Extension]

1   Factors that affect the supply of a product include

   A Consumer income levels

   B Changes in taxes and subsidies from the government

   C Changes in habits, fashion and tastes

   D The price of related goods and services

2   An increase in the price of a good will result in a .... in the .... for its complementary good, other things remaining constant.

   A Fall, demand

   B Fall, price

   C Rise, demand

   D Rise, price

3   Which factor is *not* a direct determinant of demand?

   A Price

   B Price of complements

   C Income

   D Goods and services tax

4 Determinants of supply for a product do *not* include the

   A Costs of production

   B Price

   C Technological progress

   D Consumer habits and tastes

5 A firm sells a product with a known price elasticity of demand of 0.35. What would happen to the firm's revenues of if it reduced the price?

   A Stay roughly the same

   B Increase insignificantly

   C Decrease

   D Increase

6 If products *x* and *y* have a cross price elasticity of demand value of +1.2, this means that the products are

   A Strong substitutes

   B Strong complements

   C Weak substitutes

   D Weak complements

7 Having spent an extra 12% on advertising this year, A1 Bakeries Ltd finds that sales have increased from 1,000 units per week to 1,320 units. What is the advertising elasticity of demand for A1 Bakeries Ltd?

   A 26.6

   B 2.66

   C 1.32

   D 0.75

8 The theory of supply suggests that as price increases, supply will also follow. Which statement does *not* explain why there is a positive correlation between price and quantity supplied?

   A Increased profitability attracts more firm to the market

   B As price increases, profit margins increase

   C Higher prices reduce the level of demand and therefore raises supply

   D Costs of production are more likely to be covered as prices increase

9 Which pricing strategy is most likely to apply to products with a low price elasticity of demand?

   A Skimming

   B Prestige

   C Cost based

   D Psychological

10 The cross price elasticity of demand (CED) for two products that are perfect substitutes is equal to

   A Zero

   B One

   C Infinity

   D Any negative coefficient greater than 1.0

11 The income elasticity of demand for four products is given below. Which one is most is likely to be a luxury brand?

    A -1.3

    B -0.4

    C +0.4

    D +1.3

12 Inferior goods have a ………… income elasticity of demand, meaning that demand for inferior goods ……….when income levels rise.

    A Negative, falls

    B Negative, rises

    C Positive, rises

    D Positive, falls

13 If a product has a price elasticity of demand that is greater than 1.0, then the demand for the product is said to be price

    A Inelastic

    B Elastic

    C Unitary

    D Infinity

14 Which factor below is *not* likely to allow a firm to set its prices significantly higher than its rivals?

    A It has a unique selling point

    B Its reputation or image gives it a low price elasticity of demand

    C It sells an exclusive and differentiated product

    D Price elasticity of demand for the product is high

15 Exclusivity, the feel-good factor and prestige mean that some products are actually in higher demand when the price is high. The purchase of such products is known as

    A Exclusive dealings

    B Conspicuous consumption

    C Ostentatious consumption

    D Luxury expenditure

16 Which product would *not* be classed as flamboyant consumer expenditure?

    A A Ford motor vehicle

    B An original Picasso painting

    C Nike trainers (sports shoes)

    D Gucci handbags

17 The price elasticity of demand for a product will be low if

    A A small market exists for the product

    B A large market exists for the product

    C There is a large number of close substitutes

    D There is a small number of close substitutes

18 Which of the following products is likely to have the highest value of price elasticity of demand?

    A Petrol

    B Bananas

    C Alcohol

    D Driving test

19 Which of the following products is likely to have the lowest value of income elasticity of demand?

    A Disneyland annual passes

    B Staple food

    C Ferrari cars

    D Children's books

20 Which of the following is *not* a key determinant of the value of price elasticity of demand?

    A Consumer income levels

    B Cost of raw materials and other costs of production

    C The availability and price of substitute products

    D Fashions, habits and tastes

21 The ………… the proportion of consumers' income spent on a product, the more ………inelastic demand will tend to be.

    A Lower, income

    B Higher, income

    C Smaller, price

    D Larger, price

22 What does the graph below suggest about bus travel as a service?

    A It is a normal good

    B It is a necessity

    C It is an inferior good

    D It is a Giffen good

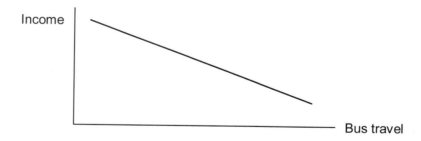

23 Which of the following products is likely to have a negative income elasticity of demand?

    A Fresh fruits and vegetables

    B Magazines

    C Personal computers

    D Frozen microwave meals

24 If the income elasticity of demand for supermarket own-label wines is -0.7, then a 5% drop in average incomes should do what to the sales of the product?

    A 3.5% fall in demand

    B 3.5% rise in demand

    C 7.14% fall in demand

    D 7.14% rise in demand

25 Products with an income elasticity of demand of between 0 and +1.0 are

    A Luxuries

    B Necessities

    C Branded

    D Inferior

26 Which type of product is most likely to be affected by an economic downturn?

    A Luxuries

    B Necessities

    C Branded

    D Inferior

27 The most ineffective advertising campaigns will have a

    A High positive AED value

    B Low positive AED value

    C High negative AED value

    D Low negative AED value

Questions 28–30 refer to a supermarket chain's sales of its own label brand of canned baked beans.

28 Suppose that the supermarket reduces the price of its baked beans from $0.40 to $0.35 per can and notices that its sales subsequently rise by 20%. What is the value of the price elasticity of demand?

    A –0.62

    B -0.71

    C -1.4

    D -1.6

29 From the above calculation, the price elasticity of demand for the supermarket's baked beans is shown to be

    A Price inelastic

    B Price elastic

    C Perfectly inelastic

    D Perfectly elastic

30 Suppose the sale of the baked beans rose from 100,000 units to 120,000 units per time period. What is the change in the sales revenue of baked beans following the given price change?

    A $20,000

    B $40,000

    C $42,000

    D $130,000

 Unit 4.5 Promotion

Task 1: Complete the missing words

Promotion is about communicating marketing messages with the intention of selling the products of a business. The main form of promotion is a.................. There are various media that can be used for this purpose, e.g. television, radio, newspapers, magazines and the I............. Promotion is important to ensure that a product has a high chance of succeeding in the marketplace. However, the spending has to be reasonable since promotion can be very expensive.

The objectives of promotion are to i.................. and to r............... customers about a firm's products and to p.................. them to purchase the products.

Promotion is often categorized as .... (ATL) or ....(BTL). ATL promotion refers to paid-for promotion, e.g. commission being paid to an advertising agency for creating a television advertising campaign. All other forms of promotion are known as BTL promotion. Unlike ATL promotion, the firm has direct control over BTL promotional activities such as: .... mailing, exhibitions, ... (POS) displays and sales promotions.

The .... refers to the different components of an individual promotional campaign. The mix may, for example, include advertising, direct marketing, personal selling and sales promotion techniques.

Task 2: Above-the-line or below-the-line promotion?

Identify whether each of the listed promotional techniques are above-the-line or below-the-line.

Promotional Technique	Above	Below
Billboard posters		
Branding		
Cinema		
Direct mail		
Free samples		
Internet		
Magazines		
Merchandising		
Newspapers		

Promotional Technique	Above	Below
Packaging		
Personal selling		
Point of sale displays		
Public relations		
Radio		
Sales promotion		
Sponsorship		
Television		

Task 3: Short answer questions

a Explain the importance of *promotion* in the marketing mix.

_____

_____

_____

_____

b Use real world examples to distinguish between *persuasive* and *informative* advertising.

_____

_____

_____

_____

c Explain why top sports clubs, such as Arsenal Football Club or Barcelona Football Club, would not want or accept sponsorship deals with a tobacco firm.

_____

_____

_____

_____

d Advise a sole trader why the use of television advertising is unlikely to be a feasible promotional channel.

_____

_____

e Outline two reasons why BOGOF (buy one get one free) deals are not feasible for most businesses or products.

_____

_____

_____

_____

f Explain the benefit of customer loyalty schemes to both the customer and the business.

_____

_____

g Despite their global dominance, why do well-established market leaders, such as Coca-Cola, Nike and McDonald's, continue to advertise?

_____

_____

h Suggest a promotional mix for a secondary school or college planning to introduce the IB Diploma Course.

_____

_____

_____

_____

_____

_____

Task 4: True or false?

		True / False
a	National television advertising is usually too expensive for most businesses to use.	
b	Advertising is another word for promotion.	
c	Pull promotional techniques rely on above-the-line promotional methods.	
d	The Internet is an example of below-the-line promotion.	
e	Direct marketing does not include media advertising.	
f	Below-the-line promotion includes: direct mail, point of sales displays and flyers (handouts).	

Task 5: Multiple choice

1 Which of the following is *not* part of promotion?
 A Advertising
 B Branding
 C Public relations
 D Price reductions

2 Below-the-line promotion does *not* include
 A Cinema advertising
 B Direct mailing
 C Branding
 D Sales promotions on packaging

3 Above-the-line promotion is
 A Any form of commercial television or radio promotions
 B The use of promotion via the mass media
 C Promotional techniques within the control of the organization
 D Used to persuade or inform customers of a firm's products

4 Firms such as Adidas, Pepsi, Police sunglasses, Gillette and Marks & Spencer use celebrities to promote their products. This is an example of
 A Sponsorship
 B Hero endorsement
 C Publicity
 D Sales promotion

5 Direct marketing is
 A Using radio, television and newspapers to sell directly to customers
 B The marketing process of selling straight to potential and known customers
 C Any form of below-the-line promotion
 D Any form of above-the-line promotion

6 Sales promotion can be best described as

  A The process of persuading people to buy a firm's products

  B Advertising using mass media to attract customers to buy a firm's products

  C Marketing techniques aimed directly as selling to the customer

  D Selling products at reduced sales prices

7 Promotion carried out through independent media such as commercial radio is known as

  A Broadcasting

  B Advertising

  C Above-the-line

  D Below-the-line

8 The catchphrase "I don't wanna grow up" is used by Toys R Us. This is an example of

  A Direct marketing

  B Above-the-line promotion

  C Corporate slogans

  D Copyrights

9 The sales method of offering a complementary product to paying customers when they purchase another product is known as

  A Free gifts

  B Complementary goods

  C Sales promotion

  D Customer loyalty schemes

10 Telesales and telemarketing are examples of

  A Direct marketing

  B Above-the-line promotion

  C Paid-for advertising

  D Homeworking

11 Which option best defines a business logo?

  A It is a registered trademark of a business

  B It is a sign or symbol that represents the products sold by a business

  C It is a sign or symbol that represents a business

  D It is a verbal representation of a business

12 Advertising strategy is least likely to consider

  A The types of media to be used

  B The costs of producing and broadcasting the campaign

  C Finance or budgetary constraints

  D Customer relations management

13 Direct mail, point of sale displays and sales promotions are all examples of

  A Direct marketing

  B Advertising

  C Below-the-line promotion

  D Above-the-line promotion

14 When an organization pays to be associated with a particular event or cause (such as the World Cup) in return for prominent publicity, this is known as

   A Charitable donations

   B Ethical marketing

   C Sponsorship

   D Financial aid

15 What is meant by 'public relations'?

   A The relationship between workers and employers

   B The relationship between customers and the business

   C Activities aimed at establishing and protecting the image of a business

   D Activities aimed at getting the business into the media

16 Using sales material such as posters and display stands to promote a product in the place where it can be bought is an example of

   A Sales promotion

   B Sales material

   C Above-the-line promotion

   D In-store advertising

17 Advertising techniques do *not* include

   A Celebrity or hero endorsements

   B Sexual attraction or appeal

   C Use of catchphrases and slogans

   D Personal selling techniques

18 Nike use Tiger Woods (golfing legend) and Manchester United Football Club, among many others, to advertise their brand. This strategy is known as

   A Mass marketing

   B Brand advertising

   C Hero endorsement

   D Product positioning

19 The choice of a medium or media to use in a promotional mix depends on several factors, but is least influenced by

   A The associated costs

   B The target audience or market segment

   C The product's position in its life cycle

   D The price elasticity of demand for a product

20 Which statement below does *not* apply to informative advertising?

   A It lets customers know about a product's characteristics, purpose and functions

   B It attempts to alert the consumer of the availability of a product

   C Focus is placed on promoting the brand or the company itself rather than a product

   D It is used by non-profit organizations to influence people's attitudes and behaviour

21 Advertisements that attempt to get customers to purchase a product are known as

   A Selling

   B Persuasive

   C Intermediary

   D Instructive

22 Advertisements that focus on promoting a business's name and image, rather than its product range, are known as

   A Branding

   B Corporate advertising

   C Own-label branding

   D Market positioning

23 The use of people to sell a firm's products directly to the customer is known as

   A Personal selling

   B Sales promotion

   C Door-to-door promotion

   D Direct promotion

24 Introductory offers, such as free installation and 3-months free viewing of satellite television, are examples of which type of promotion?

   A Above-the-line

   B Television advertising

   C Sales promotion

   D Direct marketing

25 Advantages of using television commercials compared to radio advertisements do *not* include

   A Large market coverage in diverse geographic locations

   B High audience figures from around the world

   C Attention-grabbing media that combines visual and audio effects

   D Ability to reach audiences engaged in other activities, such as when driving

Unit 4.6   Place

Task 1: Complete the blanks

Place, or ...., refers to the component of the marketing mix that deals with getting the right product to the customer in the most convenient and most cost-effective way. Firms do this through means of distribution ...., such as wholesalers, sales agents and retailers.

.... are people or organizations that act on behalf of sellers and buyers. ...., for example, are the buyers of products from a manufacturer and sell on these products in smaller units to ....

.... refers to the use of telephone calls to sell products directly to potential customers. This method has proved to be favoured by insurance and banking firms. The advantage of using this approach is that it reduces the need for sales people making personal visits, thereby saving travel time and money.

Task 2: Explain ...

a   Two advantages and two disadvantages to a customer of using the Internet to order fruits and vegetables from a local supermarket

_____

_____

_____

_____

b   The type of pricing strategy that wholesalers are most likely to use

_____

_____

c   Why a long chain of distribution is not suitable for perishable products

_____

_____

Task 3: Vocabulary quiz

Identify the key terms from the clues given. *Hint*: the answers are in alphabetical order.

Key Term	Definition
	The means by which a product gets from the manufacturer to the consumer, such as through retail outlets or distributors.
	Part of a firm's promotional mix that relies on making direct contact with existing and potential customers.
	Also known as 'placement'; the process of getting the right products to customers at the right time and place.
	Agents or firms that act as a middle person in the chain of distribution between the producer and consumers of a product.
	Specialist storage machines that stock a small range of products; can be easily placed in almost any location.

Task 4: True or false?

		True / False
a	E-commerce (business via the Internet) is a form of distribution channel.	
b	A shorter distribution channel ensures the manufacturer has more control over the marketing of its products.	
c	Cost-cutting is an important element of supply chain management.	
d	Manufacturers use intermediaries because they cannot sell directly to consumers.	
e	Distribution is one of the four main elements of any marketing mix.	
f	There are only two parties involved in a two-channel chain of distribution.	
g	Intermediation will tend to raise the marketing costs to a business.	

Task 5: Multiple choice

1 Traditional channels of distribution do *not* include

   A Retailers

   B Wholesalers

   C Warehouses

   D Agents

2 Which of the following distribution channels is most suitable for luxury products such as designer clothing?

   A Supermarkets

   B Online websites

   C Specialist retail outlets

   D Overseas markets

3 Placement in the marketing mix does *not* refer to

   A Wholesalers

   B Distributors

   C Retailers

   D Location of business

4 The channel of distribution used to sell products to an end user is known as a

   A Retailer

   B Wholesaler

   C Distributor

   D Purchaser

5 Features of a wholesaler do *not* include which of the following?

   A They have the ability to benefit from economies of scale

   B They purchase in large quantities and sell in smaller quantities

   C They charge commission for their services

   D They are suppliers to retailers

6   Which of the following is *not* an example of an agent?

   A   Travel insurance broker

   B   Financial advisor

   C   Cashier at a supermarket

   D   Residential real estate negotiator

7   Consumer durable 'white goods' (such as fridges, cookers and microwave ovens) are usually distributed using

   A   Direct marketing

   B   Retailers

   C   Agents

   D   Hypermarkets

8   Wholesalers buy products from manufacturers in large quantities and sell these onto retailers in smaller units. This service is known as

   A   Economies of scale

   B   Breaking bulk

   C   Direct selling

   D   Distribution

9   Businesses that offer online payment methods via their Internet website are using which form of placement?

   A   Direct

   B   Indirect

   C   Specialist retail

   D   Vending

10   Wholesaling is popular in which industry?

   A   Motor vehicles

   B   Bakeries

   C   Newspaper and magazines

   D   Retailing

11   Which channel of distribution trades directly with household customers?

   A   Wholesalers

   B   Distributors

   C   Retailers

   D   Vendors

12   Which statement does *not* apply to retailers?

   A   They are an intermediary in the chain of distribution

   B   They rely on the expertise of distributors and agents

   C   They deal directly with the end user

   D   They are focused on consumer markets

13 An advantage of using vending machines as a distribution method is

    A They rely on the expertise of distributors and agents

    B It is dependent on machinery working effectively

    C Sales people are not required to sell the product

    D The storage capacity of vending machines is low

14 Which distribution channel is least likely to be used by a producer of expensive products?

    A Agents

    B Retailers

    C E-commerce

    D Wholesaler

15 Which of the following is *not* an intermediary in the chain of distribution?

    A Suppliers

    B Retailers

    C Marketers

    D Agents

16 Which statement relates to the use of direct marketing?

    A Reduces the need for an intermediary

    B Costs of distribution material are minimal

    C Customers tend to read most direct mail

    D High response rates

17 **[HL Only]**   Supply chain management does *not* involve

    A Cost-cutting

    B Outsourcing

    C Increasing levels of stock

    D Logistics

18 **[HL Only]**   Supply chain management is also known as

    A Administration

    B Distribution

    C Logistics

    D Intermediation

19 **[HL Only]**   Which activity below would *not* be classed as part of a firm's supply chain management?

    A Checking the quality of supplies before distribution

    B Investigating the lowest cost distributor

    C Controlling and managing work in progress

    D Deciding on the products that are to be produced

20 **[HL Only]**   Exclusive dealings act as a barrier to entry because

    A Distribution channels are limited to a single supplier

    B Intermediation is reduced

    C Customers cannot choose the best product

    D The use of franchise agreements are restricted

Unit 4.7 International Marketing

Task 1: Explain ...

a The difference between international marketing and global marketing

_____

_____

b Why Fish and Chips, The Royal Family, Harry Potter, James Bond and The Beatles may all be examples of British cultural exports

_____

_____

c Why ethics and etiquette should be considered when a firm engages in international marketing

_____

_____

_____

_____

Task 2: True or false?

		True / False
a	Businesses need to take account of laws and regulations when marketing overseas.	
b	International marketing is also known as global marketing.	
c	The growing presence of foreign competitors has made international marketing more important to businesses.	
d	Franchising is a technique used by some firms to enter foreign markets.	
e	Cultural exports account for a small proportion of a country's GDP.	

Task 3: Odd one out

Select the odd one out from each of the options below.

a	Copyrights	Patents	Exchange rates	Health and Safety
b	Tariffs	Quotas	Embargoes	Language
c	Exporting	Joint ventures	Mergers	Takeovers
d	Interest rates	Legislation	Unemployment	Inflation

Task 4: Multiple choice

1   Difficulties faced when exporting overseas do *not* include

    A   Language barriers

    B   Cultural differences

    C   The sheer quantity of suitable customers

    D   Exchange rates

2   Which of the following is *not* a cultural consideration for international marketers?

    A   Language

    B   Local preferences

    C   Business etiquette

    D   Local laws

3   Which of the following is *not* a socio-economic consideration for international marketers?

    A   Age distribution

    B   Gender distribution

    C   Income levels

    D   Attitude towards working hours

4   The widespread use and availability of American products overseas, such as Coca-Cola beverages or McDonald's fast food, is an example of

    A   Americanization

    B   Globalization

    C   Cultural exports

    D   Free international trade

5   Natural barriers to international trade and exchange include

    A   Trade embargoes

    B   Health and Safety regulations overseas

    C   Business etiquette

    D   Import taxes

6   Businesses that benefit from being able to market their products in exactly the same way all across the world are engaged in

    A   International marketing

    B   Global marketing

    C   Marketing economies of scale

    D   External economies of scale

7   The manners and customs by which business is conducted in different countries and areas of the world is known as

    A   Culture

    B   Internationalism

    C   Business etiquette

    D   Business protocol

8 Which of the following is *not* an artificial barrier to international trade?

   A Language and culture

   B Quantitative limits

   C Embargoes

   D Customs duties

9 Opportunities of international marketing include

   A Large scale production

   B Extending a product's life cycle

   C Finding new labour

   D Marketing costs

10 Which of the following is *not* a cultural export?

   A Mobile phones from Finland

   B American pop culture

   C Japanese just-in-time production methods

   D Italian pasta and pizza meals

11 External considerations for businesses planning to market overseas do *not* include

   A Local customs and cultures

   B External sources of finance

   C International etiquette

   D Trade protectionism measures

12 Which of the following trade protectionism methods would *not* be a welcomed by foreign firms if reduced?

   A Tariffs

   B Quotas

   C Administrative procedures

   D Export restraints

13 Tariffs are taxes on ……….. goods and services and are used by governments to try to …………
   their supply into a country.

   A Imported, raise

   B Imported, reduce

   C Exported, reduce

   D Exported, raise

14 Benefits to a firm in selling products internationally do *not* include

   A Opportunities to enjoy economies of scale

   B Increased sales and profits

   C Lower prices being charged

   D Lower costs through international marketing

15 Barriers to effective international marketing include all the following except

   A Socio-economic and political differences

   B Divergence in business etiquette

   C Different legislation

   D Globalization of markets and cultures

Unit 4.8   E-commerce

Task 1: Explain ...

a   How businesses can improve their productivity *and* competitive edge by using e-commerce

_____

_____

_____

_____

b   Two drawbacks of using email in the workplace

_____

_____

_____

_____

c   How music retailers have been affected by e-commerce

_____

_____

_____

_____

Task 2: True or false?

		True / False
a	E-commerce is simply about trying to sell a firm's products via the Internet.	
b	The Internet does not necessarily provide simplicity of access for customers.	
c	High overheads can be reduced with the use of e-commerce.	
d	E-commerce has tended to reduce the importance of packaging in the broader marketing mix.	
e	E-commerce reduces the need for market research due to easier access to data.	
f	Credit card payments account for the vast majority of all online purchases.	

Task 3: Multiple choice

1 Benefits of the Internet as a medium of marketing do *not* include

    A Cheaper transactions costs

    B Cheaper transportation costs

    C Economies of scale from operating in larger markets

    D Firms have better control over their marketing

2 Which of the products below is probably *least* suited to sale via the Internet?

    A Books

    B Games consoles

    C Shoes

    D DVD movies

3 Online trading benefits a business in many ways. Which option below is the exception?

    A Opportunities to increase sales

    B Price transparency for customers

    C Provides more accurate information and updates for customers

    D Reducing overheads such as rent and insurance

4 Inappropriate and unsolicited online publicity and Internet marketing messages are known as

    A Junk mail

    B Advertising spam

    C Pop-up menus

    D Garbage in, garbage out

5 A key disadvantage of using the Internet as an advertising medium is

    A Advertising clutter

    B The costs of online advertising

    C Ability to update the advertisement

    D The potential audience size

6 E-commerce is *not* limited by which of the options below?

    A Customers may not have access to the Internet

    B Connection to the Internet can be slow

    C Security encryption can discourage online trading

    D Higher costs of overseas sales and distribution networks

7 Which of the following effects of e-commerce is a potential disadvantage to businesses?

    A Price transparency

    B Wider distribution networks

    C Display of a firm's product range

    D Choice of promotional mix

8 E-commerce has .... traditional channels of distribution whilst providing .... convenience for most customers.

    A Shortened, limited

    B Shortened, greater

    C Lengthened, greater

    D Lengthened, limited

9 Which of the following has proved to be the smallest barrier for international e-commerce businesses?

   A Set-up costs

   B Language

   C Online security

   D Costs of maintenance and technical staff

10 E-commerce is most suited to which type of industry?

   A Sunset

   B Sunrise

   C Footloose

   D Infant

11 E-commerce has revolutionized business processes. This concept is known as

   A E-tailing

   B Re-engineering

   C New product development

   D Value chain management

12 A retailer that primarily uses the Internet for trading is known as which type of business?

   A Click and bricks

   B Vendor

   C E-tailer

   D B2C retailer

13 The Internet is *least* suitable for selling which product in general?

   A Products that have attractive packaging

   B Products that have a low 'value to weight' ratio

   C Products that do not need to be tested before purchase

   D Fast-moving consumer goods

14 Social network websites such as MySpace and Facebook earn most of their money from

   A B2C trading

   B B2B trading

   C Selling advertising space

   D Online donations

15 Emailing has revolutionized how many businesses operate on a daily basis. However, it does suffer from a number of disadvantages. Which option is *not* one of these limitations?

   A It discourages face-to-face communication

   B There are high marginal costs in sending emails

   C It can reduce productivity in the workplace due to the amount of time used in checking emails

   D Spam and informal messages can clog up inboxes

UNIT

5

Unit 5.1 Production Methods

Task 1: Complete the missing words

There are several methods of production. .... production involves the output of an individual product, from start to finish, in order to meet the specific requirements of a customer. Clients are likely to pay relatively .... prices for the purchase of such products.

.... production and mass production methods both benefit from economies of scale through larger levels of output. However, the marketing mix will differ since there is less uniqueness. .... production, in particular, suffers from the standardization of output and hence relatively lower prices are charged (meaning relatively lower profit margins are earned).

[Higher Level Only]

.... production is an adaptation of line (mass) production whereby tasks are completed by teams that are given the responsibility for completing a part of the overall production process. In reality, this method of production tends to be .... intensive.

Task 2: True or false?

		True / False
a	'Production' refers to the manufacture of a physical good.	
b	Mass production is ideal for the production of homogenous products.	
c	Job production suffers from the high costs of labour intensity.	
d	Large-scale (mass) production typically involves customization of products.	
e	With flow production, when one task is finished, the next task must start immediately.	
f	Private tuition for examination preparation is an example of job production.	
g	Manufacturing output tends to be more cost effective when using labour-intensive technologies.	
h	Labour productivity can be improved by investing in better training, equipment and motivation in the workplace.	
i	Lean production methods have led to an increase in the use of job production.	

Task 3: Explanations

Randall & Taylor Clothing Co. design and manufacture trendy fashion clothing for teenagers in a variety of designs, colours and sizes.

a   Identify the production method that is most likely to be used by Randall & Taylor Clothing Co.

_____

b   Outline any two benefits that this production method brings to the company.

_____

_____

c Explain why a high level of work-in-progress is likely to mean that Randall & Taylor Clothing Co. will face liquidity problems.

_____

_____

_____

_____

Task 4: Multiple choice

1 Which of the following is *not* an advantage of job production?

   A Products can be made to customer specifications

   B Each item can be uniquely designed and produced

   C Employees may be motivated by the variety and challenge of the tasks

   D Economies of scale can be enjoyed due to the size of the project

2 All the following are involved in job production except

   A Private tutors

   B Bakers

   C Painters and decorators

   D Architects

3 Which one of the following changes would be least likely to increase the productivity of a business?

   A Greater specialization and division of labour

   B Automation that achieves technical economies of scale

   C Employing more workers

   D Using more capital-intensive production techniques

4 Which of the following is *not* a feature of job production?

   A Meets the specific requirements of a customer

   B Likely to be a unique product

   C Relatively quick to produce

   D Likely to be relatively expensive

5 Which of the listed occupations is the least labour intensive?

   A Teachers

   B Hairdressers

   C Printers and publishers

   D Painters and decorators

6 Which of the following industries is the most capital intensive?

   A Steel manufacturing

   B Consultancy

   C Fashion industry

   D Leisure and tourism industry

7 Which business is least likely to use batch production?

  A McGuiness Bakeries

  B Wong & Chan's Hair Salon

  C Robertson's Buffet Café

  D Pannu's Fruit Farm

8 Clothing companies that specialize in producing casual clothing for the general public are most likely to use which method of production?

  A Job

  B Batch

  C Flow

  D Mass

9 Mass production does *not* benefit from

  A Lower average costs of production through economies of scale

  B Stockpiling of manufactured products

  C Large volumes of standardized output

  D Use of easily recruited and trained workers

10 A feature of job production includes

  A High and stable levels of demand

  B Repetitive and boring tasks

  C High levels of output for a mass market

  D Distinctive quality and output

11 Which stage of production does operations management apply to?

  A Primary

  B Secondary

  C Tertiary

  D All of them

12 Job production is likely to have which feature?

  A Low profit margins

  B Labour intensity

  C High number of orders

  D Large economies of scale

13 Mass production does *not* suffer from high

  A Set-up costs

  B Running costs

  C Unit costs

  D Replacement costs

14 Which of the following is least likely to be standardized in the production process?

  A A bridal magazine

  B Canned soft drinks

  C School reports

  D McDonald's Happy Meals

15 Which of the following terms is *not* associated with flow production?

   A Capital intensity

   B Exclusivity

   C Production line

   D Standardization

16 What are 'idle' resources?

   A Old or outdated machinery and equipment

   B Resources that are not used cost effectively

   C Broken down machinery and equipment

   D Poor quality resources of a business

17 Which of the following is most likely to be of greater concern to a business that is deciding whether to become more capital intensive?

   A Whether there will be increased accuracy and therefore less wastage

   B Whether the investment will speed up production and increase productive capacity

   C Whether the financial returns from the investment justifies the expenditure

   D Whether the management will be able to manage the change process

18 Productivity can best be improved by

   A Paying higher wages to all staff

   B Investing in technology

   C Replacing workers with capital inputs

   D Removing an overtime policy in the workplace

19 Labour productivity will increase, at least temporarily, in the examples below. Which one is the exception?

   A Overtime work

   B Staff training and development

   C Performance-related pay

   D Using more labour intensive methods of production

20 Which of the following is *not* necessarily a disadvantage of job production?

   A Economies of scale are very limited if at all attainable

   B Production is relatively expensive and time consuming

   C Production is capital intensive

   D Highly skilled labour is used

21 Mass production does *not* involve

   A Large-scale production

   B Standardization of production

   C Using capital-intensive technologies

   D Use of a highly skilled labour force

22 **[HL Only]**   Cell production is best described as

   A Production based on capital-intensive methods

   B Production based on labour-intensive methods

   C Production process broken down into units based around teams

   D Specialization and division of labour in the production process

23 [HL Only]   When workers are organized into multi-skilled teams in the production process, this is known as

   A Assembly line production

   B Cell production

   C Compartmentalization

   D Consolidation

24 [HL Only]   All other things being equal, businesses might be more inclined to develop capital-intensive methods of production if

   A Interest rates fall

   B Wage rates fall

   C Labour productivity increases

   D Capacity utilization falls

25 [HL Only]   Which statement does *not* apply to cell production?

   A A team of workers carry out their assigned tasks

   B There is supervisory responsibility

   C There is quality responsibility

   D Employees work independently to avoid distractions

Unit 5.2 Costs and Revenues

Task 1: Vocabulary quiz

Identify the key terms from the clues given. *Hint*: the answers are in alphabetical order.

Key Term	Definition
[HL Only]	Refers to an area or department of a business that costs can be attributed to (for reasons of accountability).
	Costs that are clearly attributed to the production of a particular good or service.
	Production costs, such as loan repayments and salaries, which do not change with the level of output.
	Costs that cannot be attributed to a particular product or cost centre.
[HL Only]	Refers to a department or strategic business unit within an organization that functions autonomously and is held accountable for its own costs and revenues.
	Refers to the funds received from the sale of a firm's output.
	Refers to the aggregate amount of money spent on production for any given level of output.
	Also known as average costs, this concept is calculated by dividing the total costs of production by the level of output.
	Costs incurred directly from the production and sale of a particular product, e.g. raw materials and packaging costs.

Task 2: Calculations

a Wallets-R-Us Ltd. has fixed overheads of $500 and sells 200 units per month. Each item sells for $35 and has direct costs of $15.

  i Calculate the total costs per month for the business.

  ii Calculate the firm's profit for the month.

  iii Calculate the change in the average cost of production at 100 units and 200 units of output. Comment on why the unit cost has dropped.

b McMahon Candies has monthly fixed costs of $3,000 and unit variable costs of $2. Its current level of demand is 3,000 units each month. The average unit price is $6.

   i Calculate the firm's current average costs each month.

   ii Calculate the safety margin for McMahon Candies.

c The following data refers to the cost and revenues of Sangu Toys Ltd. when operating at 2,000 units of output per month:

Item	Cost/Revenue ($)
Price	$15
Raw materials per unit	$5
Overheads	$500
Rent	$2,000
Salaries	$3,000

   i Calculate the total cost of producing 2,000 units.

   ii Calculate the profit made by Sangu Toys Ltd. if it manages to sell all its output.

d Rhapsody Sounds produces miniature speakers with the following monthly cost structures:

Total Output (speakers)	Total Costs ($)
100	$5,000
200	$8,000
300	$11,000

   i Assuming constant unit costs, what is the value of the monthly fixed costs for Rhapsody Sounds?

   ii What is the change in unit costs of production if Rhapsody Sounds changes from producing 100 units per month to 300 units per month?

   iii If Rhapsody Sounds manages to produce and sell 200 units per month and wishes to make a 150% profit margin, what price should each unit be sold for?

Task 3: True or false?

		True / False
a	Fixed costs do not vary with the level of output.	
b	Average costs of production will fall when the level of output increases.	
c	Average revenue is mathematically the same as the price per unit.	
d	Fixed costs are those that do not change.	
e	Advertising costs tend to be considered as a variable cost of production.	
f	Economies of scale are likely to decrease the costs of production for a firm.	
g	Rent and advertising costs are considered as fixed costs for most businesses.	
h	Total contribution – Total Fixed Costs = Profit.	
i	**[HL Only]** All profit centres are also cost centres, but cost centres are not necessarily profit centres.	

Task 4: Explain ...

a   The difference between fixed costs and variable costs

_____

_____

b   Why average fixed costs will continually fall with increased levels of output

_____

_____

c   **[HL Only]**   The difference between cost centres and profit centres

_____

_____

_____

_____

d   **[HL Only]**   Why many businesses prefer to use full costing rather than absorption costing, even though the technique is less scientific

_____

_____

_____

_____

Task 5: What type of cost?

Identify the following costs for a restaurant as either fixed, variable or semi-variable in the table below.

Type of Cost	Fixed	Variable	Semi-variable
Advertising/promotional materials			
Equipment and tools			
Furniture (e.g. tables and chairs)			
Market research			
Mobile telephone bills			
Packaging materials			
Premises and buildings			
Food supplies			
Staff salaries			
Staff wages			
Utility bills (e.g. gas and electricity)			
Vehicles (e.g. delivery cars)			

Task 6: Cost and revenue formulae

Identify the category of cost/revenue from the given formulae. The first one has been done for you. *Hint*: answers appear in alphabetical order.

Type of Cost / Revenue	Formula
Average cost	Total costs ÷ Quantity produced
	Total revenue ÷ Quantity traded
	Change in total costs ÷ Change in output level
	Total fixed costs + Total variable costs
	Unit price × Quantity traded
	Unit price – Average variable cost

Task 7: Multiple choice

1   Costs which are totally independent of the level of output are known as
   A   Fixed costs
   B   Direct costs
   C   Semi-variable costs
   D   Variable costs

2   Which of the following is *not* a fixed cost for a restaurant?
   A   Bank loan repayments
   B   Waiting staff wages
   C   Air conditioning bills
   D   Rent to the property owner

3   Identify the running cost (ongoing costs) from the options below.
   A   Deposit for purchasing buildings
   B   Furniture, fixtures and fittings
   C   Interest on bank loans
   D   Licenses and permits

4   Identify the start-up cost from the list below.
   A   Raw materials purchase
   B   Packaging materials
   C   Utility bills
   D   Communications equipment

5   Which of the following items is least likely to be an expense?
   A   Electricity bills
   B   Stationery
   C   Sales
   D   Postage stamps

6   Costs that are incurred as a result of production are known as
   A   Variable costs
   B   Indirect costs
   C   Overheads
   D   Semi-variable costs

7   What can be worked out from calculating the price of a product and its variable costs?
   A   Contribution
   B   Unit contribution
   C   Break-even
   D   Profit per unit

8   Examples of variable costs for a motor vehicle manufacturer do *not* include
   A   Costs of raw materials
   B   Piece-rate payment systems
   C   Insurance costs
   D   Costs of component parts

9   If a firm's average costs are falling, then its marginal costs must be
   A   Increasing at a faster rate
   B   Falling too and at a faster rate
   C   Falling too but at a slower rate
   D   Constant

10   As the production level of a firm increases, which cost will fall continuously?
   A   Costs per unit
   B   Average Variable Costs
   C   Average Total Costs
   D   Average Fixed Costs

11 Overheads are best described as

   A Costs that vary with the output level in the short run

   B Costs that are fixed in the short run

   C Costs that must be paid to generate output

   D Costs from non-operating activities

12 If you were given the 'Average' (e.g. Average Cost), which other variable would be required to determine the 'Total'?

   A Contribution

   B Quantity

   C Currency

   D Unit of measurement

13 If a product has a selling price of $10, average variable costs of $4, and a sales volume of 1,200 per period of time, then the total contribution is

   A $6

   B $4,800

   C $7,200

   D $12,000

14 If a firm has total costs of $2,000 and fixed costs of $1,100 for an output level of 600 units, then the average variable costs must be

   A $0.67

   B $1.50

   C $1.83

   D $3.33

15 Study the table below and determine the fixed costs of production for the firm.

Output	Variable Cost $	Total Costs $
10	1,500	3,845
15	2,250	4,595

   A $750

   B $1,500

   C $1,595

   D $2,345

Unit 5.3   Break-even Analysis

Task 1: Complete the missing words

Break-even occurs when a firm's ……….. revenues equal its ……….. costs. The firm will make a ……….. if it operates below its break-even level of output. By contrast, if it is able to generate more revenue than costs incurred in production then it will make a ……….. Profit is the positive difference between revenues and the ……….. of production, i.e. Total Revenues less Total Costs.

In order to calculate break-even, it is common to use the ……………... method by dividing the ……….. costs by the difference between the product's selling price and its variable costs of production. For example, if a manufacturer of wooden toy trains has fixed costs of $3,000 per month, with an average variable cost of $10 and a selling price of $25, then its break-even level of output would be ……….. trains per month.

Task 2: True or false?

		True / False
a	Cutting price will mean more sales and therefore a firm can break even quicker.	
b	The margin of safety can be negative.	
c	As the price of a product increases, the break-even level of output will fall.	
d	When variable costs rise, the break-even level of output will fall.	
e	When total costs rise, the margin of safety will fall.	
f	If selling price is $10, unit variable costs are $4 and fixed costs are $9,000 then the break-even level of output is 1,400 units.	
g	A weakness of break-even analysis is that firms may have to, in reality, lower their prices to sell more.	
h	The usefulness of a break-even analysis depends on the manager's accuracy in predicting costs, revenues and production levels.	

Task 3: Calculating break-even

Smash Racquets Co. makes a profit of $10,000 on sales revenue of $50,000. Its fixed costs are $5,000 and sales volume is 1,000 units per month. Calculate the following for Smash Racquets Co.

 a   Selling price

 b   Variable cost per unit

 c   Break-even level of output

 d   The margin of safety if Smash Racquets Co. expects to sell 600 units per month

Questions 3e and 3f refer to the following information.

Fit-it Tyres Ltd. has fixed costs of $100,000. Its average selling price is $30 with unit variable costs of $15. Use this information to calculate its:

e Unit contribution

_____

_____

f Break-even level of output

_____

_____

g Complete the missing labels in the break-even chart below.

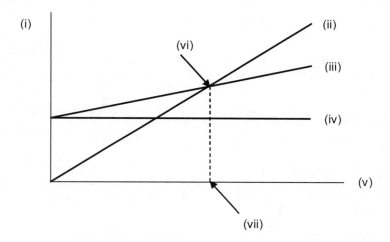

h Explain why it is difficult to construct a break-even analysis for a multi-product firm.

_____

_____

i Outline two causes of a fall in a firm's margin of safety.

_____

_____

Task 4: Multiple choice

1 Which of the following is *not* a direct cost of production for a car manufacturer?
   A Raw materials
   B Wages of production workers
   C Factory rental costs
   D Depreciation

2 A premium hotel can raise its revenues in a number of ways, except for:
   A Reducing fixed costs
   B Reducing its prices
   C Reducing labour costs
   D Raising prices during peak periods

3   Which of the following is a strength of break-even analysis?

    A It assumes that all the output is sold

    B It accounts for variances in actual sales and planned output

    C It assumes that all output is sold at one price

    D It accounts for both fixed and variable costs

4   Contribution per unit is calculated by ………… price minus the ………… variable costs.

    A Average, Total

    B Total, Average

    C Selling, Average

    D Average, Total

5   Total contribution is the difference between

    A Total revenue and total variable costs

    B Total revenue and total costs

    C Price and total costs

    D Price and variable costs

6   Which of the following costs will continually decline for a taxi driver as the mileage covered increases?

    A Total Variable Costs

    B Total Fixed Costs

    C Average Variable Costs

    D Average Fixed Costs

7   Any output sold ……… the break-even will generate a ………….. for a business

    A Near, Loss

    B Above, Profit

    C Above, Loss

    D Below, Profit

8   Contribution per unit is calculated by using the formula

    A Price less average fixed costs

    B Price less average variable costs

    C Total revenue less total costs

    D Total revenue equals total costs

9   A firm has total sales revenue of $5 million with sales of 4,000 units. Its average costs are $600. Fixed costs are $1 million. What is the total contribution for the business?

    A $1.6 million

    B $2.4 million

    C $2.6 million

    D $3.6 million

10 If a business raises its price, which of the following is most likely to occur

    A Break-even output will fall

    B Profits will increase

    C Profits will fall

    D Break-even output will rise

11 Which of the following is a direct cost to a computer retailer?

   A Marketing costs

   B After-sales care

   C Rental costs

   D Depreciation of delivery vehicles

12 Which of the following statements apply to the concept of 'margin of safety'?

   A The margin of safety can be increased if a firm becomes more liquid

   B The firm produces at the break-even level of output so is financially safe

   C The firm operates at a level higher than its break-even

   D The firm makes neither a profit nor a loss

Questions 13–16 refer to the following information.

Parc Oasis Ltd. has fixed costs of $15,000 per month, with average variable costs of $200 and a selling price of $500 per unit.

13 What is the total cost of production to Parc Oasis Ltd. if it produces 100 units each month?

   A $15,200

   B $15,700

   C $35,000

   D $65,000

14 What is the average cost of producing 200 units per month?

   A $275

   B $500

   C $40,000

   D $55,000

15 What is Parc Oasis Ltd.'s break-even level of output per month?

   A 21

   B 30

   C 50

   D 75

16 If Parc Oasis Ltd. wanted to earn a profit of $50,000 on the sale of 100 units per month, what selling price should be set by the firm?

   A $500

   B $575

   C $700

   D $850

Questions 17–20 refer to the following information.

Jade Villa offers holiday accommodation at a beach resort. It has fixed costs of $22,500 per time period. The variable cost per letting averages at $250.

17 If the average villa is let out (hired) for $1,000, how many villas must the firm let out to break even?

    A 23

    B 25

    C 30

    D 32

18 What is the value of Jade Villa's total revenue at the break-even point?

    A $22,500

    B $25,000

    C $28,500

    D $30,000

19 If the firm hires out 50 villas per time period, what is the average cost per letting?

    A $250

    B $450

    C $700

    D $1,000

20 If Jade Villa planned to earn a contribution of $1,000 per letting, what price should it charge, on average?

    A $1,000

    B $1,250

    C $2,000

    D $2,275

21 [HL Only] Which of the following is *not* an assumption of break-even analysis?

    A Variable costs per unit are constant

    B Economies of scale can only occur as the firm expands output

    C Productivity levels are held constant

    D Forecasts are only as goods as the data used to make the predictions

22 [HL Only] A key limitation of break-even analysis is that

    A It is a static model that does not cater well for the dynamic nature of business

    B Average fixed costs are very difficult to calculate in reality

    C It cannot allow for changes in fixed costs of production

    D Calculating the desired contribution at different sales levels is cumbersome

23 [HL Only] Which of the following is *not* a criticism of using break-even analysis?

    A Costs are unlikely to be linear in reality

    B Unit costs are unlikely to remain constant across all levels of output

    C Prices are unlikely to be constant across all levels of sales

    D Multi-product firms cannot use break-even analysis

24 [HL Only]   Break-even analysis can help in the following business decisions, except for

    A   Make or buy decisions

    B   Special order decisions

    C   Risk assessment

    D   Qualitative decision-making

25 [HL Only]   The concept of break-even is used in which investment appraisal technique?

    A   Payback period

    B   Accounting rate of return

    C   Discounted cash flows

    D   Net present values

Unit 5.4 Quality Assurance

Task 1: Complete the missing words

Quality assurance (QA) requires the implementation of processes and systems to make certain that quality standards are met to ensure customer s...................... QA is used by a business to give its customers greater confidence in the quality of the products that they are purchasing from the firm. A firm that is able to meet QA standards will publicize this, usually with the use of quality assurance trademarks, e.g. ISO ....

At the heart of QA are concepts such as lean production and .........-.......-.......... (a production system that eliminates the need to use buffer stocks by having stocks and components delivered as and when they are needed in the production process). QA also involves all members of an organization striving to make small, continuous adjustments and improvements. This philosophy is known as ...., the Japanese term for 'change for the better' or 'continual improvements'.

One other way used by businesses to achieve QA is by comparing their practices or performance indicators with those of the best in the industry. This technique is known as .... (or simply 'benchmarking' for short). BPB allows businesses to develop plans and strategies, based on best practice, in order to improve their .... Benchmarking is as a continuous process in organizations that make every effort to achieve quality assurance.

Task 2: True or false?

		True / False
a	Quality means that a product is high-class and one of the best in its industry, such as Rolls Royce cars or Rolex watches.	
b	Kaizen and Zero defects are central principles of any total quality culture.	
c	The 'Kitemark' is a quality assurance standard recognised throughout the world.	
d	Quality is a source of global competitiveness.	
e	Poor quality means that a firm's prices are higher than the industry average.	
f	An objective of quality assurance is to reduce the need for huge Research & Expenditure spending.	
g	The implementation of TQC tends to reduce the level of employee motivation.	
h	Kaizen usually involves the implementation of quality circles.	

Task 3: Explanations

a   Explain how each of the following cases outlines poor quality:

   i   Poor customer service at the cinema

   ii A laptop that keeps breaking down

   iii Food that is overcooked in a restaurant

_____

_____

_____

_____

_____

b Explain which of the following is least likely to be a measure of quality:

    i Reliability

    ii Staff turnover

    iii Maintainability

    iv Safety

_____

_____

c Explain two costs to a firm that strives to achieve quality assurance.

_____

_____

_____

_____

d Explain one advantage to a washing machine manufacturer that is accredited with international QA certification such as the ISO 9000.

_____

_____

Task 4: Multiple choice

1 The customer's perception of product quality is ultimately measured by

    A Price

    B Image

    C Value for money

    D Excellence

2 Which benefit does *not* apply to lean production?

    A Reduced costs of holding stock

    B Fewer mistakes being made

    C Flexibility in meeting sudden changes in demand

    D Improved quality assurance

3 Which of the following is *not* a method of lean production?

    A Quality Circles

    B Just in time production

    C Mass production

    D Kaizen

4 Which of the following is *not* a method of waste minimization?

    A TQM

    B JIT

    C Quality circles

    D Recycling

5   A feature of total quality management is

   A High production levels

   B Zero defects

   C Social responsibility

   D Altruism

6   Which of the following concepts is *not* associated with lean production?

   A JIT

   B TQC

   C MBO

   D TQM

7   The effect of substandard quality includes

   A Higher levels of customer services

   B Improved customer relations

   C Higher wastage levels

   D Lower costs of production

8   A product that serves its purpose in fulfilling a customer need or desire is known as

   A Fit for purpose

   B Quality assurance

   C Class excellence

   D Commercial honesty

9   The use of traditional methods to inspect quality against required standards is known as

   A Benchmarking

   B Yardstick

   C Quality control

   D Command and rule

10 Which of the reasons below does *not* explain why quality is important to a business?

   A Quality is essential in order to satisfy customers

   B Quality can provide a competitive advantage to the business

   C Quality raises the goodwill of the business

   D Quality means less stress to employees due to the reduced workload

Unit 5.5   Location

Task 1: Complete the missing words

The location decision is highly important for a business because it has a direct and long-lasting impact upon a firm's ...., revenues and therefore its .... Good location decisions require in-depth research and analysis of the costs and .... of different sites, taking both quantitative and .... factors into consideration.

Task 2: True or false?

		True / False
a	Firms may choose to locate overseas to exploit lower costs of labour.	
b	Allowing foreign firms to locate in the domestic country is harmful to the economy as there will be unemployment.	
c	The time and cost of transportation is considered by managers to be more important than distance.	
d	The location decision is irreversible.	
e	High sunk costs can be a key reason for deterring relocation decisions.	
f	Assisted areas suffer from a lack of employment opportunities.	
g	Ethics do not have a purpose when making international location decisions.	

Task 3: Explain two reasons why ...

a   The cost of land in city centres is higher than that in more remote locations

_____

_____

_____

_____

b   Government grants and subsidies may be available to businesses that locate in areas of low income or high unemployment

_____

_____

_____

_____

c   The Internet has made the location decision less onerous for many businesses

_____

_____

_____

_____

Task 4: Multiple choice

1   Which of the following is least likely to affect the choice of location for a business?

   A   Infrastructure such as access to motorways, railways and ports

   B   Availability and quality of land and hence its rental value

   C   Financial incentives such as tax allowances and government subsidies

   D   The need for physically meeting with customers

2   Weight-losing businesses locate near the source of raw materials in order to

   A   Benefit from economies of scale

   B   Reduce transportation costs

   C   Benefit from easy access to customers

   D   Gain from mass production

3   Which of the following would *not* attract a business to a particular area?

   A   Nearness to market

   B   Nearness to raw materials

   C   External economies of scale

   D   Internal economies of scale

4   The location decision for a 'footloose business' does *not* depend on

   A   Cost of the site

   B   Government grants and incentives

   C   Access to labour

   D   Proximity to the market

5   Which of the firms below would be classified as a weight-losing business?

   A   Sanda's Bouncy Castles

   B   Lewis & Stott Bakeries

   C   Reed Oil Company

   D   Chen Motor Manufacturing Company

6   Access to air transportation is considered better than access to rail or water transport for the hauling of which product?

   A   Durable products

   B   Expensive products

   C   Bulky products

   D   Dangerous products

7   Rail transportation is most suitable for the transportation of

   A   Heavy, bulky and durable items

   B   Large expensive products

   C   Perishable products

   D   Items of great urgency

8   For businesses such as hypermarkets, wholesalers and manufacturers of mass-produced cars, the most important consideration when choosing location is

   A   The cost of land

   B   The proximity to customers

   C   The proximity to raw materials

   D   Infrastructure

9   A footloose business is one that

   A   Cannot gain any cost advantage from a particular location

   B   Benefits by relocating from place to place to benefit from access to different markets

   C   Benefits by relocating from place to place to benefit from access to raw materials

   D   Moves from one country to another

10   Government incentives for location or relocation do *not* include

   A   Grants and subsidies to reduce costs of production

   B   Low or interest-free loans to encourage investment

   C   Taxes imposed on harmful by-products to protect the local community

   D   Training and development programme for the local workforce

11   Which of the following is a qualitative factor affecting the location decision?

   A   Availability of land

   B   Transportation costs

   C   Labour costs

   D   Nature of infrastructure

12   Which of the following is *not* a quantitative factor affecting the location decision?

   A   Availability of highly skilled workers

   B   The cost of land

   C   Management preferences

   D   Government financial assistance

13   The international location decision is least likely to be affected by issues regarding

   A   The stability of exchange rates

   B   Industrial inertia

   C   Language and cultures

   D   Traditions and etiquette

14   When businesses locate near other organizations that function in similar or complementary markets, this is known as

   A   Competitor analysis

   B   Aggregation

   C   Infrastructure

   D   Clustering

15   What is the term used to describe the benefits that have been established over time due to a firm's presence in a particular location?

   A   Economies of scope

   B   Acquired benefits

   C   Enterprise zones

   D   First-mover advantage

Unit 5.6   Innovation

Task 1: Complete the missing words

Innovation refers to the introduction of a new process, product or idea. .... refers to the process by which an innovation is accepted and adopted by the market.

In order to provide inventors with an incentive to innovate, the legal system will control and enforce the use of intellectual property rights, such as c...................... and t...................... People wishing to use any copyright material or a registered trademark must first seek the legal permission of the copyright holder. .... give an entrepreneur or a business the exclusive and legal right to produce a new product or to use a particular production process. Intellectual property rights are recorded on a firm's ...., under the section of intangible assets.

Task 2: True or false?

		True / False
a	Copyright is legal protection for written pieces of work, such as literature, to protect the property rights of the creator.	
b	Innovation usually stems from creativity.	
c	Tasters are often used to entice early adopters of a product.	
d	Making modifications or improvements to existing products is known as product research.	
e	Expenditure on research and development leads to higher sales revenues.	
f	Research and development expenditure is justified in sunset industries.	
g	Operating in an unfilled niche market is an example of innovation.	

Task 3: Explain ...

a   Why direct marketing is more suitable than television advertising for marketing products to 'innovators'

b   Why Research and Development is usually a prerequisite to the successful launch of a new product

c   Two limitations of innovations to a firm with limited market share

d   Two sources of innovation

Task 4: Multiple choice

1   Innovation refers to

A   The development of new ideas and working practices

B   The commercial development and use of an invention to appeal to consumers

C   New products being developed on the market

D   Market-orientated marketing

2   One purpose of spending huge amounts of money on research and development is

A   To increase earning potential of the business in the future

B   To gain rights to patents or copyrights

C   To eliminate competition

D   To diversify a firm's activities

3   Which of the following would *not* qualify to be protected by copyrights?

A   Radio broadcast

B   Hollywood movies

C   Photographs

D   Medicines

4   The group of people who are willing and financially able to try anything because of the novelty factor (the product is new) is called

A   Innovators

B   Imitators

C   Initiators

D   Early adopters

5   The group of people who are typically the last to buy a 'new' product is called

A   Late majority

B   Laggards

C   Slackers

D   Bargain hunters

6   Benefits of innovation do *not* include

A   Growth opportunities

B   Productivity gains

C   Brand switching

D   Reduced product failure rate

7   Which of the following is *not* a constraint of innovation?

A   High costs

B   Budgetary constraints

C   High failure rate

D   International competitiveness

8   Which type of innovation refers to changes in the way that production takes place?

A   Process innovation

B   Product innovation

C   Cost reducing innovation

D   Incremental innovation

9 Which of the following is the least likely long-term benefit to a firm that is innovative?

  A Growth opportunities

  B Unique selling point

  C Brand loyalty

  D Improved competitiveness

10 Research and development is unlikely to feature which concept?

  A Test marketing

  B Prototypes

  C Position mapping

  D Market research

11 Research and development expenditure is often used as a barrier to entry by large businesses that dominate the market. What are these firms collectively known as?

  A Pure monopolists

  B Oligopolists

  C Adversaries

  D Monopsonists

12 A newly invented process or product that is legally and exclusively assigned to the producer is known as a

  A Intellectual property right

  B Patent

  C Copyright

  D Trademark

13 German car manufacturer Volkswagen uses the 'VW' logo as part of its marketing. What does this represent to the company?

  A An invention

  B A patent

  C A copyright

  D A trademark

14 In which financial accounts do companies record their intellectual property rights?

  A Balance sheet

  B Profit and loss account

  C Cash flow statement

  D Appropriation account

15 Drastic and extensive innovations that involve high risks to a business are known as

  A Crisis innovation

  B Incremental innovation

  C Radical innovation

  D Riotous innovation

Unit 5.7 Production Planning

Task 1: Complete the missing words

Production planning involves managers overseeing and controlling the level of stock in a business. Stocks can come in three forms: r...... ...., w.........-.........-..............., and f................. .... The .... (EOQ) is the level of stock that minimizes the firm's average costs. Firms need to balance the costs of holding large volumes of stock with the drawbacks of holding insufficient quantities of stock.

Delays in the .... (the period of time taken for a supplier to process and deliver a stock order) will mean that stocks fall below the desired minimum level and the firm has to rely on its .... stock.

.... stock control systems rely on the use of buffer stocks in order to meet changing levels of demand. By contrast, ... systems have stocks delivered immediately the moment that they are required for production. This helps to improve the firm's working capital since money is not tied up in stocks (which might not be highly liquid).

[Higher Level Only]

.... is increasingly being used by businesses to reduce costs by contracting out activities to external firms and agencies. These third party organizations possess the skills and know-how to supply products in a more cost-effective way.

Task 2: Explain ...

a The difference between just in case (JIC) and just in time (JIT) stock control systems

_____

_____

b [HL Only] The probable effect on the organizational structure of a firm that subcontracts a significant portion of its operations

_____

_____

c [HL Only] How it is possible to outsource production internationally yet keep the business growing domestically

_____

_____

d [HL Only] The difference between outsourcing and offshoring

_____

_____

e [HL Only] Suppose a firm has fixed costs of $100,000 and a productive capacity of 50,000 units per month. Calculate the change in the average fixed costs of production if the firm operates at only 85% capacity compared to operating at full capacity

_____

_____

_____

_____

Task 3: Interpreting JIC stock control diagrams

a   Identify the five missing labels in the diagram below.

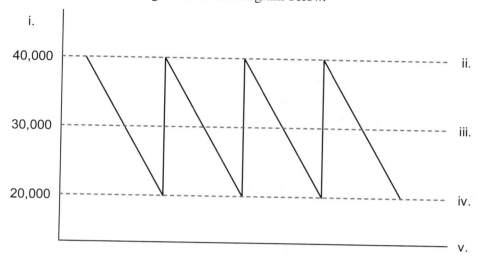

b   Identify the:
  i   buffer stock
  ii   reorder quantity
  iii   reorder level from the above diagram.

Task 4: Multiple choice

1   Which of the following is *not* a type of stock for a business?
  A   Work-in-progress
  B   Raw materials
  C   Ordinary shares
  D   Finished goods

2   Costs of a stock-out do *not* include
  A   Loss of sales
  B   Disgruntled customers
  C   Negative impact on cash flows
  D   Storage costs

3   Stockpiling means that a business
  A   Operates at a level lower than its buffer stock
  B   Produces on a larger scale to benefit from cost savings
  C   Builds up excessive levels of inventory
  D   Plans for a safe safety margin

4   A drawback in holding too much stock is

    A   Stocks are highly liquid assets

    B   Inflexibility in production levels

    C   Working capital is tied up

    D   Share prices are likely to drop due to excess supply

5   One drawback in outsourcing operations to overseas firms is that

    A   They might have a more skilled labour force

    B   They might have lower costs of production

    C   The quality of production may be more difficult to monitor

    D   Geographical distance becomes a major communication barrier

6   Productive efficiency is *not* usually measured by using which of the following measures?

    A   Labour turnover

    B   Unit costs of production

    C   Output per worker

    D   Output per machine hour

7   One advantage in using a just-in-case stock management system is that

    A   There is flexibility to meet sudden changes in demand

    B   Buffer stocks can be minimized

    C   Stockpiling is less likely to occur

    D   Productive efficiency is encouraged

8   The stock handling method based on having stocks being delivered only when they are needed is known as

    A   Reorder levels

    B   Just in time

    C   Just in case

    D   Usage rate

9   The automated system of stock management that reorders stocks as and when they are required is known as

    A   CAD-CAM

    B   OCR recognition

    C   EPOS

    D   Spot checks

10   JIT does *not* suffer from which limitation?

    A   Total reliance on third-party suppliers

    B   High administrative costs

    C   Inflexibility in meeting unexpected changes in demand

    D   Higher levels of wastage and reworking

11 The rate at which stock levels are used up in the production process is known as

   A Usage rate

   B Reorder rate

   C Reorder quantity

   D Lead time

12 The production level that allows a firm to benefit from minimal unit costs of production is known as the

   A Buffer stock

   B Economic order quantity

   C Economies of scale

   D Kaizen

13 Which incident might cause a firm to have to rely on its buffer stocks?

   A Lower costs of production

   B Sudden increase in demand

   C Timely deliveries from suppliers

   D Shorter lead times

Questions 14 and 15 refer to the diagram below for Atkinson Farms Ltd.

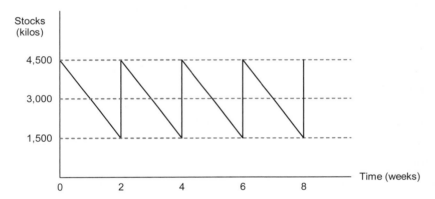

14 What is the lead time for Atkinson Farms Ltd?

   A 8 weeks

   B 6 weeks

   C 2 weeks

   D 1 week

15 What is the reorder quantity of Atkinson Farms Ltd?

   A 4,500 kilos

   B 3,000 kilos

   C 1,500 kilos

   D zero

16 **[HL Only]**   A disadvantage of low capacity utilization for a firm is

    A   Higher indirect costs of production

    B   Higher average fixed costs of production

    C   Higher fuel and energy bills

    D   Overtime payment to staff

17 **[HL Only]**   If a firm's maximum productive capacity is 35,000 units per month but it actually produces 28,000 units per month, then its capacity utilization is

    A   125%

    B   80%

    C   25%

    D   20%

18 **[HL Only]**   Firms with …. profit margins and …. levels of break-even will benefit from high capacity utilization.

    A   high, high

    B   low, low

    C   high, low

    D   low, high

19 **[HL Only]**   Capacity utilization for a business facing high growth rates could be improved by

    A   Holding lower levels of stock

    B   Reducing lead times

    C   Using JIT stock control

    D   Subcontracting work

20 **[HL Only]**   A danger for a restaurant operating at full capacity is that

    A   Food quality will fall

    B   Queuing times will rise

    C   Working capital will be stretched

    D   Staffing costs will rise

21 **[HL Only]**   What is the term given to the practice of reassigning business operations to an external firm in order to improve cost effectiveness?

    A   Offshoring

    B   Subcontracting

    C   Delegating

    D   Contractual fringe

22 **[HL Only]**   The exception to reasons for businesses in using offshoring is

    A   Workforce flexibility

    B   Reduced costs of production

    C   The use of specialist labour

    D   Consideration and observation of overseas regulations

23 [HL Only]   Which of the following is *not* a quantitative method that can be used to help with 'make or buy' decisions?

 A Break-even analysis

 B Investment appraisal

 C Cost-benefit analysis

 D Ratio analysis

24 [HL Only]   Subcontracting does *not* benefit from

 A Lower unit costs of labour

 B Greater labour flexibility

 C Greater job security

 D Improved labour productivity

25 [HL Only]   The outsourcing of business activities to an external agency or third party that is located overseas is known as

 A Outsourcing

 B Offshoring

 C Internationalizing

 D Subcontracting

Unit 5.8   Project Management

Task 1: Complete the missing words

Network analysis (or .... analysis) is a management decision making tool. It is generally used for routine tasks for which the .... (or time) of each activity is known. It is important to determine all the .... needed to complete the project and to identify all interdependent tasks. In order to improve operational ...., tasks which can be carried out simultaneously are also identified. Once the network for the project is constructed, the .... path can be identified to show the best course of action to take without delaying the .... of the project.

Task 2: True or false?

		True / False
a	The duration of activities in critical path analysis are not drawn to scale.	
b	There is no float time on the critical path.	
c	The critical path determines the shortest time possible that is needed to complete a project.	
d	The first stage in any network analysis is to estimate the completion time of each activity.	
e	The float is the amount of time that an activity can be delayed without affecting the duration of the whole project.	
f	Network analysis helps managers to allocate resources needed to execute a project.	

Task 3: Constructing a network

Complete the missing numbers in the network below and identify the critical path.

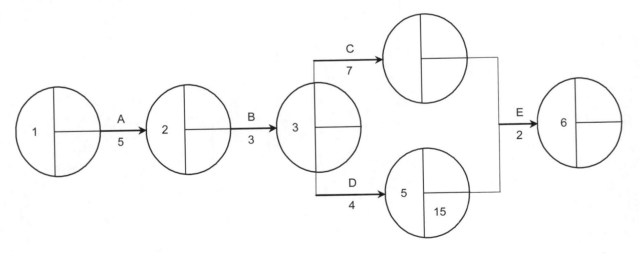

Critical path = ...

Task 4: Multiple choice

1 Which of the following is *not* used to construct a critical path analysis?

   A Duration of activities

   B Dependencies

   C List of all activities

   D Cost of activities

2 Network analysis is *not* so useful for

   A Decisions that rely on quantitative measures

   B Routine projects with minimal uncertainty

   C Projects with uncertainty in completion times

   D Large projects with a long sequence of activities

3 Activities that have a float

   A Show the shortest possible time needed to complete a project

   B Can be delayed without prolonging the project

   C Cannot be delayed without making the project longer

   D Cannot be started in conjunction with other activities

4 The key advantage of CPA is that it

   A Helps managers to focus on the most important activities and to devote resources accordingly

   B Reduces the risks of conducting business

   C Quantifies decision making

   D Eliminates wastage in activities

5 Consequences of delays in a project do *not* include

   A Higher costs and hence loss of profits

   B Financial compensation paid to customers

   C Lower staff morale

   D Higher labour turnover

6 The earliest finishing time (EFT) is calculated by

   A The earliest start time for the activity plus the duration required to complete the activity

   B The latest start time for the activity plus the duration required to complete the activity

   C The earliest start time for the activity minus the duration required to complete the activity

   D The latest start time for the activity minus the duration required to complete the activity

7 What is the name given to the period of time between an activity's earliest and latest start time (or between its earliest and latest finish time)?

   A Slack

   B Lag

   C Delay

   D Setback

8 Section ii in the diagram below refers to the

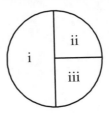

   A Earliest start time

   B Earliest finishing time

   C Latest finishing time

   D Latest start time

9 What is the value of the free float for activity C in the diagram below?

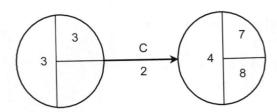

   A 2

   B 3

   C 5

   D 6

10 Which of the following statements is *not* a disadvantage of network analysis?

   A No amount of planning can guarantee that projects go smoothly and according to plan

   B Failure to identify certain activities in a project will render the critical path void

   C The critical path is only valid if all input data is correct, accurate and up to date

   D It does not promote operational efficiency as much time is consumed in planning

UNIT 6

Unit 6   Business Strategy

Task 1: Strategic tools

a   Porter's Five Forces Analysis

Identify the competitive force from the given clues:

Force	Description
	The extent to which rival goods and/or services are available, and their relative price, desirability and quality.
	The purchasing power of customers in the industry.
	The nature of barriers to entry to an industry, i.e. how easy (or difficult) it is for new firms to enter the market.
	The degree of competition between firms already in the industry.
	The market power held by suppliers, vendors and subcontractors to the industry.

b   The Marketing Mix

Identify the correct element of the marketing mix (price, product, promotion or place) from the given examples of marketing strategy for a fast food restaurant. An example has been done for you.

Element of the Marketing Mix	Marketing Strategy
Promotion	Sponsors local sporting events
	Wider menu options
	Free home delivery service
	'Kids eat free' campaign
	'Early bird' discount
	Eat for half-price on Tuesdays
	Secures celebrity endorsement contract

c   The Boston Matrix

Match the strategy with the categories in the Boston Matrix:

	Product Category		Strategy
A.	Cash Cow	X.	Avoid, minimize or liquidate to improve cash flow
B.	Dogs	W.	Either sell off or invest in very heavily
C.	Stars	Y.	Low investment due to low growth
D.	Question marks	Z.	Invest to hold or improve market share

Task 2: True or false?

		True / False
a	Strategic management covers the activities of all functional areas of a business in order to achieve organizational objectives.	
b	Strategic management is an ongoing process.	
c	Strategic management provides overall direction to the staff of an organization.	
d	A strategic business unit (SBU), with responsibility for its own strategy, operates totally independent of the overall organization.	
e	Strategic business decisions are made at all levels of an organization.	
f	Contingency plans allow a business to be better prepared to manage a crisis.	
g	Opportunities and threats refer to the external forces that a business might face in the future.	
h	Routine decisions are also known as tactical decisions.	
i	The key strengths of an organization by which strategy is built upon are known as core competencies.	

Task 3: Multiple choice

1   The art of formulating, implementing and evaluating key decisions that enable a business to achieve its objectives is known as

   A Operational management

   B Strategic management

   C Tactical management

   D Management by objectives

2   Which of the following statements does *not* apply to business strategy?

   A Evaluates cross-functional decisions

   B An ongoing process

   C Considers changes in the external business environment

   D Follows a consistent and systematic methodology

3   Which stage is *not* part of the strategy formulation process?

   A How we will get there

   B Where we are now

   C Why we want to be there

   D Where we want to be

4   Which of the following tools is least likely to be considered for strategic planning?

   A Decision trees

   B PEST analysis

   C Time series analysis

   D Ansoff's Matrix

5 When evaluating business strategy, which criterion is unlikely to be used?

   A Acceptability

   B Suitability

   C Feasibility

   D Responsibility

6 The suitability of a business strategy can best be evaluated by the use of which business tool?

   A Decision trees

   B Boston Matrix

   C Perception mapping

   D Fishbone analysis

7 Which of the following management tools is based on qualitative analysis?

   A Investment appraisal

   B Cash flow forecasting

   C Break-even analysis

   D Stakeholder mapping

8 The pursuit of best practice in an industry is known as

   A Force field analysis

   B Competitor analysis

   C Benchmarking

   D Re-engineering

9 Which of the following refers to Porter's generic strategy of focusing on high volumes of standardized production to benefit from economies of scale?

   A Cost leadership

   B Differentiation

   C Focus

   D Segmentation

10 Internal growth strategies include

   A Exportation

   B Diversification

   C Vertical integration

   D Franchising

UNIT **7**

Unit 7   Student Bloopers

What is wrong with each of the following statements? *Note*: these are real statements from students.

1   "The cash flow cycle is used to calculate whether or not a business is running on a profit or a loss."

_____

_____

2   "… but cutting wages could lead to a bad corporate culture".

_____

_____

3   "I believe that the firm should raise the cost of their services slightly because …"

_____

_____

4   "Another fixed asset for the firm is patents of their catering equipment."

_____

_____

5   "The cash balance fell as the firm took out an overdraft and therefore has to pay back it debts."

_____

_____

6   "The balance sheet shows that the firm has purchased 100% more stock."

_____

_____

7   "However, shareholders would not be pleased about the increase in taxation; the amount paid has gone up by over double."

_____

_____

8   "Even though the overall profit has gone up by 248%, the costs and expenses of the company have also risen."

_____

_____

9   "The firm has 2 dogs (in their product portfolio) so they are losing money."

_____

_____

10 "Extension strategies can be used to help revive the cash cows."

_____

_____

11 "The employees' morale would drop because they know that the firm is doing poorly meaning they might get sacked."

_____

_____

12 "Large companies like Cathay Pacific can use price skimming… as they have a good brand… so people are willing to buy their tickets for a high price."

_____

_____

13 "Economies of scale is where big firms can benefit by buying in bulk…"

_____

_____

14 "One advantage of a partnership is that it is easy to set up with only a Deed of Partnership needed."

_____

_____

15 "One advantage of a partnership is that the work can be split equally between the partners."

_____

_____

16 "If the opening balance in January is $500 and the sales revenue in January is $600, then the total cash inflow is $1,100."

_____

_____

17 "Some firms borrow a lot of money to cover its costs and sometimes even if they seem to make profit, they may still owe the bank a lot of money and therefore (are) not really making profit."

_____

_____

18 "Raising prices means that demand for the product will fall therefore there would be less sales revenue."

_____

_____

19 "Raising prices means less demand, but the sales give more profit hence reduce the break even point."

_____

_____

20 "As long as a customer's order, such as a special order decision, is profitable then the company should take the order."

_____

_____

21 "GDP refers to total spending by a country's citizens, i.e. the total spending of all households."

_____

_____

22 "Multinationals are firms that operate in more than two countries."

_____

_____

23 "Investment means the same as saving money."

_____

_____

24 "High price elasticity of demand means that as price falls, people will buy more."

_____

_____

25 "To increase market share, a firm can offer Buy One Get One Free deals."

_____

_____

26 "To sell more, a firm can advertise their products on TV."

_____

_____

27 "Large firms benefit from economies of scale, which means lower costs as a firm sells more."

_____

_____

28 "To sell more, a firm can reduce its prices, and therefore as people buy more then profits will go up."

_____

_____

29 "Takeover is when a business obtains full management control over another business as a result of purchasing over 50% of its share capital."

_____

_____

30 "Diseconomies occur when a firm suffers sales in a recession so their average costs increase."

_____

_____

31 "If the Consumer Price Index falls, that means prices have fallen."

_____

_____

32 "Supply of oil falls, so the price increases. This will therefore cause demand more scarce."

_____

_____

33 "... demerit goods such as pollution"

_____

_____

34 "Monopolies can charge whatever price they want."

_____

_____

35 "McGregor's motivation theory can be classed as Theory X and Theory Y."

_____

_____

o increase as oil is

_____

_____

_____

_____

_____

_____

_____

_____